FORBIDDEN BEHAVIOR

Pearl K. Stone

DISCLAIMER

This is a work of fiction. It is inspired by true events. However, all character names, business names, etc., are not real. Any similarities to persons, living or deceased, or events are fictional.

ACKNOWLEDGMENTS

This book is dedicated to my grandmother Ruth and my sister Sophia who battled cancer. Thank you for the help and encouragement that you gave me while you were present on this earth. You will never be forgotten and will always be in my heart.

I know that you are in a better place. I hope that I have made you both proud.

I would also like to thank my cover illustrator, Leroy Jones, for creating something beautiful that conveys Naomi's story.

AUTHOR AUTOBIOGRAPHY

Pearl is a resident of Virginia. Her passion for helping others continues to grow through being an advocate for women and children in crisis as well as helping individuals with disabilities. She is a leader at her church and mentors teenagers and young adults. Pearl is an animal lover and currently has one furry friend whom she adores. In her free time she enjoys event planning and creating designer floral arrangements with her unique gift of design and style.

Pearl was inspired to write Forbidden Behavior through some of her life experiences and hopes to inspire others to open up and find their strength.

FOREWORD

This is the story of an innocent child born into difficult circumstances. Her experiences were hard, and she went through things that no child should. Naomi's story is inspired by true events. Overcoming trauma and abuse is one of life's hardest challenges, the desire to end it all might seem like the only option, but it isn't. Find something good, a feeling, a person, or a goal and hold on to it. Taking a step into Naomi's world is tough, but her experiences are a sign that you can change your circumstances. Don't give up; know your worth and have faith. You are not alone!

CONTENTS

CHAPTER 1

NEIGHBORHOOD

I woke to the sound of birds chirping. It was cheerful, and the sun crept through the crack in my curtains. This was always my favorite time of day; everyone was waking up and getting ready for whatever activities they had planned for the day; the breeze was still cool, and the sun peeking through my curtains held the promise of a day filled with games and outside activities. I could hear Lightening barking, and my smile fluttered a bit. Lightening was our dog. We lived on a large piece of land with trees lining the yard, pecan, peach, pear, apple, and even a berry vine. Lightening was tied up in the yard; his job was to scare off any potential thieves.

At the tender age of nine, my heart couldn't handle seeing him tied up there. I wanted to grab his leash and take him for a walk so that he could see the neighborhood instead of being stuck to his pole all the time. The one time I tried, Mom warned me; she smacked my fingers and said that Lightening would yank my arm clean off if I untied him. He was much

1

bigger than me, so I resorted to sitting with him when I could and petting his soft, black fur. I'd often volunteer to take his food and water to him. He looked so lonely out there, but he was a good guard dog, and no one had ever broken into our yard. I think he was too intimidating to those who thought about it.

We lived in a small neighborhood. Everyone knew everyone in Maryville, which wasn't a terrible thing. Our neighbors were friendly, and people were always willing to help if you needed anything. It was a middle-class area, and, just like anywhere, it had its ups and downs. Mostly nosy neighbors and a few that had more money, so they believed they were better than others. I didn't like those people; just because you have lots of money didn't mean that you are a better person. Grandma always taught us to be kind, help where we could, and listen where we couldn't. I tried to do that, but sometimes it was hard.

Mom had her hands full raising us, I was the oldest of five, and even though we were far from well off, we had never missed a meal or lacked anything that we needed. We lived right next to my grandma and grandpa; they owned the house that we lived in, and it was great having them so close. Mom appreciated the help, especially since we were five youngsters. We didn't have a dad; Mom never spoke much about him except to tell us that he was selfish and didn't want us. I vaguely remembered him, but he had left once my last sibling was born, so we never knew him, and he certainly never helped Mom raise us.

When I walked out of the back door to give Lightening his water and put a bit of Vaseline on his ears to prevent the flies from landing on them, I felt giddy that the sun was out and it was warm. These were the best days, everyone played outside, and the old folks sat on their porches, soaking up the sun. I had a few friends in our neighborhood, but I'd often play on my own. Having brothers and sisters made you appreciate the calmness of being on your own sometimes. I'd put on my favorite sundress; it was white with big sunflowers on the front, my feet were always bare, though, and I'd tried to pull my hair up in a ponytail, but I had never been able to get it neat and straight. Mom was too busy to help me with girly things like that, so I looked at how other girls did it and tried it on my own. I wanted to paint my nails and put pretend makeup on like my friends, but I didn't want to ask Mom to show me. The last time I asked her, she just about shouted my head off, and I spent the afternoon crying in the bathroom.

I sat with Lightening for a while, patting his head and giving him treats that I'd snuck out of the pantry. Suddenly I heard a raucous. Ms. McGee was standing by our fence; she was drunk again, and the fence groaned and clanged with the way she held onto it. Grandma hated Ms. McGee because she was always drunk and making a nuisance of herself. It was almost as if Ms. McGee enjoyed pushing Grandma's buttons. Most days, it was funny, Ms. McGee always did the weirdest things when she was drunk, and she had the biggest potty mouth out of all our neighbors.

As I watched, my jaw dropped when the old lady started to lift her skirt. *Oh no! She was going to pee in our garden again!* It may have come as a shock to most people, and I would not have believed it myself if I hadn't seen it before, but when Ms. McGee got really drunk, she would stumble over to our fence and pee right into our garden. This morning she was in fine form, it wasn't even 10 AM, and she was already completely drunk. I could almost smell the whiskey from my seat next to Lightening and crinkled my nose. I had no idea why adults drank. I tasted Mom's wine once a while ago; she'd fallen asleep in front of the TV, and I snuck up and took a sip. I always saw her drinking the dark red stuff, and curiosity got the best of me. It was horrible, sweet but bitter, and it burned all the way down my throat. I had to run to the bathroom before coughing my lungs out.

Otherwise, I'd wake Mom up, and I knew I would get a beating if she caught me drinking her wine.

I jumped up and ran into Grandma's house. "Grandma, she's doing it again!" I yelled as I stumbled through the screen door.

Grandma looked down at me, a little dazed. "What's that, girl?"

"Ms. McGee, Grandma, she's going to pee in the yard again!" I said breathlessly.

At that, Grandma was up and out of the door in a shot, faster than any old lady I'd ever seen. I followed to see what would happen. Grandma's face was red, and she looked like she was going to climb right over the fence and clobber Ms. McGee.

"You put those skirts down, woman! Don't you dare pee in my yard!" Grandma shouted; her cheeks were flushed, and her hair blew in wisps around her face. "There are children here; they don't need to see that. It's disgusting."

Ms. McGee stumbled a bit and laughed. "I will pee where I want to, Beep Bop or whatever they call you, you old bat!" I wanted to laugh, but I held it in. I knew Ms. McGee wasn't herself; it was the alcohol inside of her that made her character change. Beyond wanting to laugh, I also felt sorry for her.

Grandma bent and took her slipper off her foot. "Oh no, you will not." She grumbled as she pulled the shoe behind her head. The first one hit Ms. McGee right on the arm, and before she knew it, Grandma was on her with the second shoe. Grandma smacked Ms. McGee until she retreated into her own house. "That's right, go home and pull yourself together, woman. And don't even think about coming close to my yard again!"

Ms. McGee mumbled something under her breath, and Grandma went to collect the shoe that she had launched at that woman.

I tried my best not to laugh at what had just happened. I knew very well how painful those shoes felt when they connected with flesh. Grandma was ruthless, but she was also a kind and generous woman, especially with my siblings and me. She would discipline us if we were naughty, but she'd make sure to show us love after. She was one of my favorite people.

I spotted Donald and Erin across the street. They were my two younger brothers and made it their mission to annoy me. They were giggling at Grandma and Ms. McGee's still retreating figure as I walked over to them. They spotted me and asked me to play with them, but I wasn't in the mood. My heart sank when they asked again, but I still refused. It wasn't that I didn't want to, but I was uncomfortable, the giggles and laughter from the incident with Ms. McGee now gone. Something had happened the previous Saturday, and I was still trying to figure out why I felt so ashamed. It had been my dark, little secret since, and I couldn't bring myself to tell anyone; just the thought of it brought tears to my eyes. Instead, I filled my time with Lightening and drawing pictures, helping Grandma with anything she needed, and whatever else I could find to keep myself from thinking about it.

The previous Saturday had been a day much like this one. It was hot, and most of the children went to play in the open field nearby. We played hopscotch, double dutch, a few rounds of hide 'n' seek, and any other games we could think of. As the day went on, I started feeling irritated, the insects were flying into me, and my clothes were dirty, two things that I didn't like when I went out to play. *These darn bugs! I just want to play!* I swatted at the buzzing insects that kept flying into my arms and face. I stomped my foot in frustration. The other kids didn't seem to mind them, they just kept playing, but I felt sweaty and tired, so every time they flew into me, I felt even more bothered.

As I looked around, I spotted one of Mom's friends, Blair, watching me. He had been around for a long time and always brought orange slices when it was hot like this. He was around Mom's age and came to the house to visit her sometimes, and everyone loved him. He was always friendly, and sometimes he would bring a big bag of candy for me and my siblings to share. Mom never knew about the candy; she didn't like us eating sweets and sugar because it made us hyper. I waved at Blair, and he motioned for me to come over; one last glance at my friends, and I ran to him. He had a red popsicle in his hand, and my mouth drooled at the sight of it.

"Hey Naomi, you look a little irritated out there." He smiled and handed me the popsicle, and I closed my eyes in pleasure as the ice-cold liquid ran down my throat. It was finished in a few seconds, much to Blair's amusement.

"The bugs are making me crazy. They always fly into me when it gets so hot, and I hate it." I crossed my arms in frustration.

Blair giggled and nodded. "It is very annoying. Well, why don't you come inside for a bit? We can watch a movie, and maybe when you come back out, the bugs will be gone. It's much cooler inside, too. I have the cooler running. Plus, I have a whole freezer full of those red popsicles."

It sounded very tempting; I was sweating, and my dress was so dirty. I thought of an ice-cold glass of water, and my mouth watered. I grinned up at him and nodded; the red popsicles were my favorite, after all. He opened the gate of his fence, and I walked inside. I had never been inside his house, and it looked a bit messy. There were takeout packets on the kitchen counter, an ashtray, and empty beer cans on his coffee table, and it looked like smoke hung in the air. I wrinkled my nose at the smell, Mom smoked in the house, and the TV room always smelled like smoke. I knew I'd never smoke, it smelled terrible, and I often listened to Mom cough throughout the night.

Since we didn't have a father figure in the house and Mom spent most of her time at work, I never knew that it was wrong to go into a man's house alone at such a young age. Even if you know someone, it could still be dangerous. I was a lot more aware of that now. Since Blair was gentle and kind, I never expected that he would change my life in a bad way.

Blair made some popcorn and grabbed a big jug of sweet tea, the ice clinked against the glass, and I couldn't wait to drink my fill. He led the way downstairs into his den, and the TV was huge in my 9-year-old eyes. It was much bigger than ours, for sure. I jumped up on the couch and smoothed my dress over my knees. Blair sat next to me and handed me some tea; I swallowed it in two big gulps. I felt a little less tired as the cold sweetness ran down my throat and cooled my body. The cooling in the house was lovely; goosebumps decorated my arms as the breeze chased the heat from outside away.

"Oh my, you are a thirsty little thing, aren't you?" He laughed and licked his lips, his gaze stuck on me.

I giggled and nodded while he poured another glass. I shifted into the soft cushions on the couch and bounced my legs happily. I couldn't remember what movie we watched, but it was funny. I remember both of us laughing at what was happening on the screen. Every time I looked at Blair, he stared at me, and I started to feel a bit uncomfortable. He was sitting quite close to me, and every now and then, I would shuffle away from him.

After the movie was finished, I was ready to play again, so I stood up and dusted the popcorn remnants from my dress. I drank the last bit of my third glass of sweet tea and smiled at Blair in thanks.

"Where are you off to, missy?" Blair asked as I moved around the couch.

"I want to go and swing on the tire outside. Thank you for the movie!" I said and turned to the stairs.

Blair shifted to the edge of the couch. "Why don't I swing you in here? It will be a lot more fun, and you won't need to worry about the bugs or the dirt."

I hesitated for a second. I felt uneasy, but I really didn't like those bugs, and Mom would be furious if I got any more dirt on my dress. So, I shrugged and walked back over to Blair. He took my hands and swung me around in a circle a few times, and then, when I thought I would burst from laughing, he flung me into the air and caught me. It was fun, and my tummy hurt from laughing so much. Blair threw me into the air a few more times and eventually stopped. He was red in the face. At nine years old, I was petite for my age, but even then, it must have been exhausting throwing and catching me. I flopped onto the couch. Blair poured the last of the tea into our glasses, and he finished his in one big gulp.

"Do you want to play horsey?" Blair asked; he was breathing hard.

I looked at him with furrowed brows. "What's that?"

"Come here; I'll show you." He said with a laugh and stretched his hand out to me.

My hand was tiny in his; his hands were massive and warm. He held on a moment too long, and the unease returned. I hesitantly allowed him to pull me to him. Blair placed me on his leg, so I was straddling it, with one leg on either side of his knees. I pushed my dress down, and Blair grabbed my hands and held them in front of me like the reins on a horse. He started hopping his knee up and down, and I bounced along with the movement; it was funny, and it really did feel like riding a horse. My sisters and I had gone horse riding once before. It was so much fun. Since that day, I had really wanted a pony, but Mom would never get me one. Grandma took us riding when she had extra time and money, especially when we were particularly well behaved.

Blair bounced faster and faster, and I was a bundle of giggles in a matter of seconds. He then turned me around so that I was no longer facing him. He carried on bouncing, and I had to hold onto his knee for balance. He had his hand on my waist, and with every bounce, he moved me closer to him. I barely noticed until I felt something hard press against my backside and thigh between his legs. At that time, I had no idea what it was. I felt uneasy, but I didn't say anything since I had no idea what was happening. Blair's pace started to slow down; he shifted me against it more and continued bouncing at a slower pace. I was still laughing, but it was more uncomfortable now. The air in the room seemed to change; it became heavier and darker. After a few moments, Blair went quiet and shuddered behind me. His hand gripped my waist harder and then let go. He let out a deep breath, and I didn't know why, but tears sprang to my eyes.

When I climbed off and thanked him for the games, he was out of breath and leaned on his knees as he smiled and nodded at me. I left the house and couldn't shake the uncomfortable feeling. I didn't know what happened, but somehow, whatever it was, it felt wrong. I never played close to Blair's house again, and I didn't see him around. I felt dirty and like I had done something I wasn't supposed to even though I hadn't done anything.

The following year in school, I learned what that hard thing between his legs had been, and I felt so ashamed. Blair had rubbed his erection against me, and I felt like a piece of innocence had been ripped from me. I couldn't understand why Blair would do such a thing. After sexual education class, I knew why it happened, but it was only supposed to happen to adults when they loved each other and not with a child. My face grew red as the anger and shame washed through me.

For a long time after that, I blamed myself; I felt like I had caused it. I was angry that I hadn't known that it was wrong, that Mom hadn't taught me anything about these things. I needed to know. I didn't play with the other children in the field again. I avoided Blair completely; even when he came to visit Mom, I stayed in my bedroom or in the bathroom so that I didn't have to see him. For most of my younger years, it had plagued me. I felt stupid and naive; I didn't trust other men around me for a long time, especially if they were older, and I never spoke about Blair and what had happened.

Why me? Why did he have to do this to me? I feel so dirty, so betrayed.

It was all I could think of for a long, long time. I think I lost most of my childhood at that point. I lost the fun-loving, caring little girl I had been before Blair. I felt mistrust for the first time, and it never really left. I always wondered if people had an ulterior motive for wanting to spend time with me.

Years later, I saw Blair again. He had become a clergyman in church. My stomach had coiled at the sight of him. He was much older; the golden-brown of his hair had faded to a dull brown with patches of grey, he had a belly, and he wore glasses. That morning he waved at me, he motioned for me to come over, but I ignored him. I wondered if he remembered what he had done, I wondered if he felt guilty or if he wanted to apologize, but that would mean acknowledging that he did something wrong first, and I'd learned that people don't like to admit it when they are wrong. Did he ask God for forgiveness? That's the question I desire to know.

As for me, that was unfortunately not the last time a piece of my innocence was stolen.

CHAPTER 2

MOM

Mom was a busy woman. She worked most of the time, so as I got older, I started taking care of my younger siblings. It was hard, and I felt like I missed out on just being a child, but I knew she needed help, especially with five children. She was nothing like Grandma. Where Grandma was hard but still loving, Mom was a lot less loving, and as we got older, the small amount of love that she did show disappeared. She started expecting the help instead of being appreciative of it, and it felt like sometimes she forgot that I was a child.

One evening, I was cooking for the family while Mom was at work. I learned how to cook at a really young age because Mom was usually out late. Grandma taught me, and we spent many evenings in the kitchen. I loved cooking, but I wasn't very good at it until years later when I knew what flavors went with certain foods. I loved experimenting. It was late, and she hadn't come home yet, which was strange because she usually came home before dinner was made. We had all just sat down at the table to eat when a knock on the door startled me. I opened the door, and my cousin, Shelly, stood there; her cheeks were flushed, and she looked slightly panicked.

"Where is everyone? I need to talk to all of you." Shelly said breathlessly.

"We're all at the dinner table; we were about to eat. What's wrong?" I could feel the tension in the air, and it was making me nervous. I hated bad news, and from the look on her face, this looked like bad news. Shelly was the only cousin that came to visit. We didn't really get along most of the time. She was in her teen years and didn't have time for us, so her being here was strange.

Shelly pushed past me, and after a heartbeat, I followed her into the dining room. My brothers and sisters all looked up in excitement, but their smiles faded when they looked at the expression on Shelly's face. It was the first time they had all been completely quiet in a very long time, the last time was when Mom got a call from our dad, and we all wanted to hear what they were talking about. Mom caught us eavesdropping and shooed us to our rooms before we could hear any part of the conversation.

Shelly cleared her throat, and I sat down in my chair. "Something happened to Aunt Estell, your mom, I mean. There was an attempted robbery when she left work, and she was shot." There was a collective intake of breath around the table. "Now, it wasn't bad, but she has been taken to the hospital. The doctor said she would be okay; she's just in shock."

I felt tears well in my eyes, and as I looked around, the tears were mirrored in each of my siblings' eyes. Except for Donald, he had always been harder when it came to bad or sensitive situations. It was strange, but I had never seen him cry, even when Mom smacked him for being naughty. Donald had the nerve to ask which arm was injured.

"It was her left one, Donald." Shelly gave him a strange questioning look and turned back to us. "I'll be staying with you until she comes home from the hospital." She disappeared for a few moments and came back with a bag in her hand. She then went into the sitting room, where she laid out a pillow and blanket on the longest couch. I wanted to offer her my bed, but I didn't think she would be too happy sharing the room with my younger sisters, and I couldn't think about anything but Mom at that point.

The next three days were filled with keeping the house clean, getting everyone ready for school, and cooking. I was exhausted by the third day when Mom came home. We were all extremely happy to see her again, and when we heard the door of the truck slam, all five of us raced to the window to watch her come in. Grandma was helping her up the path to the front door. Her left arm was in a sling, and it was tucked into her side like a bird that had injured its wing. Mom looked like she hadn't slept at all, there were dark circles under her eyes, and she slouched a bit. When she walked inside, I made sure to keep my siblings from barreling into her with excitement.

"Hi Mom, we're so happy you're back. We missed you! How are you feeling?" I asked. I wanted to hug her, but even before the attack, she had never been very affectionate, so I decided against it. I could count on one hand how many times she had hugged me since I was a baby.

She smiled at us. It was tight and didn't reach her eyes, but it was something. "I'm okay, Naomi. I hope you all behaved and listened to Shelly."

Shelly and I nodded. "There were a few tantrums, but we managed to keep the house standing and in clean shape."

"Does it hurt? Did they get the bullet out?" I asked. I couldn't help myself. I wanted to know if the doctor had managed to remove the bullet and how they would have done it.

"No, they had to leave the bullet in my arm."

"Why?"

Mom took a deep breath as if to steady herself. "The doctor said it would hurt me a lot more if they took it out."

My brows furrowed in confusion. "That doesn't make sense, though. Wouldn't your body heal if they took it out?"

"No, it was too close to a main nerve in my arm, and if they had operated and damaged the nerve, then there was a high possibility that I wouldn't be able to use my arm, so he left it there." She said as she hobbled toward her bedroom.

Everyone followed her; they were still asking if she was okay and if she was in pain. Mom waved us off and disappeared into the room. She slept for hours and hours. I sat outside her door for a while. She was moving around a lot; I could hear the bedsheets crackling with every move. Our cousin left after getting dinner ready for us. She asked me to tell Mom that she had left dinner for her in the fridge. I was happy and sad to see her go. During the three days, Shelly had barely spoken to us, but she helped around the house. It would be a lot harder to do everything on my own.

It was times like these that I realized how badly I wanted a father figure in the house. We weren't supposed to take care of ourselves, let alone each other. I wished that my dad would one day decide to come home so that I didn't have to be a mom to my siblings. I didn't feel like a child anymore, and after the robbery, Mom expected me to keep doing the things I had done while she was in hospital, like cooking and cleaning, getting my siblings bathed and dressed for school. It felt very unfair, but the robbery changed Mom. She'd always been strong and brave, but now she was gripped with anxiety and fear. Her constant bad mood started trickling down to everyone else. We were arguing a lot more, and my youngest siblings threw more tantrums. Home just didn't feel the same anymore.

The fear carried on for months. She was terrified of going to the store or anywhere in public. She was worried she would be attacked and shot again. Mom stopped working because she couldn't face going to the place where she had been shot again, so we relied on the goodwill of our neighbors to survive. We often had our dinner at Grandma and Grandpa, but we had to cut down on meals a lot. They were some of the worst months of my life. Grandma and those close to Mom tried to convince her to get help, and to see a therapist, but Mom's pride was still intact in that sense. She didn't want to admit that she was struggling or that she needed help, and for a while, I was convinced that we would have to live off other people for a long time. What happened when their goodwill ran out? We would most definitely end up on the street.

When Mom finally faced her fears and decided to work again, she started to work in a different industry than what she was in before. She completed her culinary studies and managed to get a part-time job as a prep chef. It wasn't enough to keep us afloat, so Mom had to find more work, and eventually, she was back to hardly ever being at home. She left just after we were up and came home after bath time, so we didn't get to spend much time with her. It didn't seem to bother her at all since I did all the chores. Once again, I made sure my siblings and I had food and that they got ready for school in time, and then I would help with homework and do the bedtime routine. I was exhausted every day and fell asleep in class a few times, but I was determined not to let my brothers and sisters suffer. If I slacked off, Mom would yell at me or punish me by not letting me out on weekends.

After some time juggling multiple jobs, Mom put Erin, my youngest brother, in a private school, which sparked jealousy in all of us. We all knew that Erin was the favorite. They say parents never have a favorite child, they should love all their children equally, but that isn't true. Erin never got into trouble, he was spoiled, and he was the only child to go to a private school. Erin could do no wrong in Mom's eyes, and it created such a bitter feeling in my heart, especially when he started acting like he was better than all of us.

I felt so alone and frustrated. *When will I be noticed?* I cook, I clean, I babysit my siblings, but Mom never even gave a hint of appreciation. Instead, she only commented on the things that weren't to her standard. If the kitchen wasn't clean enough or the washing wasn't done when she got home, she scolded me in front of the others. I wanted to live with Grandma, but I knew it would be too much. Grandma had already raised children of her own. She didn't have the money or the time to raise another. Besides, if I left, there would be no one to take care of my siblings. The anger in me grew daily. I didn't have friends because I was at home all the time, and I never played anymore either. I couldn't remember the last time I laughed or made jokes. I couldn't remember the last time we had a day without arguing or fighting.

Mom started drinking more, and she would often be mean to us. We all teased her behind her back when she got drunk, like when we would call her sasquatch because she would stumble around on her massive feet. This was only funny until one of us caught her attention, and then she would spew mean words at us. Mom never told any of us that she loved us, except Erin. We weren't entirely sure what love was, and even growing up, we had to learn through other relationships. I couldn't say *I love you* to anyone else well into my adulthood because we never learned that it was normal or

19

something that was needed in a healthy relationship. It was incredibly hard, feeling like we were just disappointments to Mom when she never spoke nicely to us. As I grew up, I realized that Mom was filled with anger, hatred, and jealousy, and I never knew what we had done to make her feel that way. Perhaps she regretted having so many children or being alone, and she took those emotions out on us. As the drinking got worse, Mom started dating different men, a few of them appeared to be drunks, and when she brought them over, I made sure that I locked our doors. I didn't know the men, but I knew that we weren't always completely safe, especially when Mom drank until she passed out on the sofa or on the floor. Whenever that happened, the men would stumble around the house looking for more beer or whatever alcohol was available. There were many times when I had to roll Mom out of her own puke and then try to clean her up as best I could. She didn't listen to anyone. She didn't listen to Grandma and most certainly not to me, so I continued trying to do the best that I could. All the while losing the childhood that I should have had.

I knew she had mental issues, and as a teenager, I would try to convince her to get help and to speak to someone, but she would just yell at me and tell me to mind my own business. After a few years, I just stopped trying to help her. She just sunk deeper and deeper into her black hole. Mom wasn't always this bad. There were times when I was much younger, before a few of my siblings were born when she joked and played around with me. Before the alcohol and the incident with the shooting, she had moments where she showed that she cared, not with her words but with her actions. Even though she worked long hours back then, when I helped at home, she would say thank you or buy me candy or chocolate and sneak it to me so that the others didn't notice. I missed those days, but as time passed, the memories started to fade until I wasn't sure if they were real anymore.

Mom's family was small; it consisted of Grandma and Grandpa, a few cousins, and her sister. We never met our aunt, the only connection we had to her was Shelly, and if that was any indication, I doubted that I would like my aunt either. Grandpa was a very quiet man; he kept to himself and rarely paid attention to us. Whenever we went there to visit Grandma, he would retreat to their bedroom and read or do whatever else he enjoyed. Grandma always said he was a hard man. His parents weren't very loving, so he didn't know how to love them. I could see the similarities between Mom and Grandpa, and on many occasions, I wished that Mom could be more like Grandma.

On rare occasions, Mom would make us breakfast or dinner when she had a little extra time, but that also ended when she started drinking. All the extra money went into drinks; she never spoiled any of us. By the time I was a teenager, the temptation to run away was overwhelming. There was a constant dark cloud hanging over our family, and I could feel the start of depression even before I became a teenager. I didn't speak to anyone about it, including Grandma. I made a point of dealing with it alone. Back then, mental health wasn't something that many people cared about, people didn't believe in depression or anxiety, and you were told to get over it. I felt completely isolated, and my life went by in a haze of cooking, cleaning, and mothering.

I wanted to shake Mom and beg her to be her old self, to just be our mother again, but I didn't dare.

CHAPTER 3

MIDDLE SCHOOL

"Get up, get up, get up!" Mom's voice rang through the house. "It's 7 AM; you're late!"

I groaned; I hated school. "Do I have to go, Mom? Can't I just have a sick day?"

"Don't be absurd, Naomi. Get your brothers and sisters ready. Breakfast is in the kitchen." She turned on her heel, leaving me to handle the kids.

I was a little shocked that she'd made breakfast this morning. After a moment's pause, I got dressed and helped Donald, Erin, Marsha, and Jackie. They all rushed to the kitchen while I finished up in the bathroom.

"Naomi! Hurry up; you need to eat!" She shouted again.

I rolled my eyes and huffed, "I'm coming; I'm just finishing up!"

I could smell the bacon and eggs, and my stomach growled at the sight of the grits. I glanced at the clock on the wall and grabbed my lunch bag. Another surprise, Mom had prepared our lunch as well. Today was bound to either be a good day or a really bad day.

"I'll have to miss breakfast, Mom; I have a long way to walk, and I'm going to be late if I stay for breakfast." I plucked an apple out of the fruit bowl and made my way to the door. I wanted to stay, just to see Mom sober for a few more minutes. Maybe this time, it would last longer.

"Okay, make sure you cook early tonight."

I didn't respond. I always made dinner at the same time every evening. As I walked the few blocks to school, I enjoyed the breeze and listened to the birds chirping. I loved walking to school. It was tiring, but I loved the sounds in the morning and the sunlight that pierced through the leaves in the trees. I spotted a Blue Jay and smiled at the beautiful song it was singing. *It must be nice to be so free, to fly wherever you want to.* The butterflies were fluttering past me, and for a few moments, I forgot about everything bad. I wanted the day to be good, it had been so long since I'd enjoyed just any normal day, but I promised myself and God that I would do my best to stay positive for the day.

The happy feeling disappeared when I got to school. I hated it; it had never been pleasant for me. I was bullied for the way I looked—my skin was extremely fair, and I had long dark hair and brown eyes. It didn't help that I was petite as well. But what bothered me the most was being bullied because of my skin tone. Kids at school would tease me and call me names like ghost girl or anything else that hurt. I tried to keep a straight face and not let them see when a comment bothered me, but I spent a lot of time crying in the girls' bathroom in between classes. The bullying got worse as I got older.

I mostly kept to myself, so when I got threats of fighting after-school, it would take me by surprise. Kids would just come up to me and accuse me of being full of myself. It completely baffled me, and a lot of the time, I was scared that someone would physically hurt me. I couldn't understand why kids were so mean for no reason or for the way I looked or acted. I'd spent many days crying after school from the mean things that were thrown my way. I wanted to stand up for myself, but I knew the principal would call Mom, and then it wouldn't matter who was wrong; I would be punished for inconveniencing her. I often sat and prayed to God, asking Him why people were so horrible. I prayed for strength to get through the days at school and for the strength to not let their words hurt me. I looked forward to summer. When I didn't have to return to this horrible place for a little while, it was all that kept me going.

That morning, I made it to Ms. Shelton's English class just as the bell rang. She was tall and slim and wasn't hesitant to dishing out discipline when the students misbehaved in her class. I was the last to walk into the classroom, and she raised her left eyebrow at me. I mouthed an apology, made my way to my assigned seat, and groaned internally when I saw my nemesis behind me. I wished we had the choice of changing seats; then, I could avoid being targeted by her every day.

It was Sarah Macary, 135 pounds of pure evil, and she hated me for some reason. Sarah was the school's biggest bully.

She stood at 5'7," and her face was dotted with acne. Her golden tanned skin and dark hair made her seem even more intimidating.

Her icy gaze was fixed on me as I took my seat. She had a reputation for bullying anyone that wasn't up to her standard, but for some reason, it seemed like I was right at the top of that list. Every year since she started at my school, she'd gone out of her way to make my life difficult, and my quietness seemed to encourage her.

Why me? Why can't I just get one day, one good day, with no issues at home or at school? I tried to ignore Sarah, figuring that would be the best way to avoid being her target for the day. Sometimes it worked. Sometimes it made the invisible target on my back even bigger. I wished I had the confidence to tell her off, but I didn't want to get into trouble. I'd worked hard to be a top student no matter what went on at home, and I made sure to stay up after my siblings were sleeping to do my homework. Mom didn't care much for my high grades, but I motivated myself with the goal of one day being able to make enough money to take care of myself and others in need.

"Alright, class, let's settle down. I don't want any talking this morning. We have a lot to cover today, and I don't want to waste any time. Please send your homework forward." Ms. Shelton moved to each row of seats and collected the homework sheets.

Sarah was trying to say something to me, and as I turned around to ask her what she wanted, Ms. Shelton looked over at me. I whipped my head back around and ignored the sniggering from Sarah.

"Naomi, didn't I just say no talking?"

My heart rate picked up as she put her hands on her thin hips. Her lips were pursed, and the usual look of disappointment made her eyebrows furrow. Other students had often been the recipient of that glare, but this was the first time that it was trained on me.

"I... I wasn't talking, Ms. Shelton. It was Sarah. I just turned to find out what she was saying and tell her to keep quiet." I stuttered over my explanation.

She looked at Sarah over my shoulder. "Is that true, Sarah? Were you talking?" She'd moved back to the front of the class, hands still firmly on her hips.

"No, ma'am, it was Naomi. She's lying. I told her to keep quiet." She said sweetly. Ms. Shelton sighed, and Sarah had a self-satisfied look stuck on her face.

Anger boiled up inside of me, I don't know why I was surprised that she blamed me, but I couldn't get my anger under control. I wanted to smack the look off her face. Ms. Shelton motioned with her finger to me and pointed to the hallway; my heart sank. I tried to explain again, but she wasn't having any of it. Head down, I made my way to the hallway, where I had to lean up against the wall. We called this the Wall of Shame, and it was where Ms. Shelton handed out discipline. I never misbehaved, and I had never experienced the Wall of Shame. I couldn't understand why Ms. Shelton didn't believe me; I was one of her best students. She should have weighed up my performance with the likelihood that I would misbehave, and then she would have realized that Sarah was wrong and that she was lying. Sarah deserved this punishment more than I did.

I put my hands against the wall and bent slightly so that my backside stuck out. She held her brown paddle in her hand and pulled her arm back; the first one was the worst. The holes in the wood somehow made the impact more painful, and I wanted to cry. She gave me five hard smacks with the paddle; the sound reverberated through the empty hallway, and by the time she stopped, it felt like my behind was on fire. I wanted to cry, I wanted to let the tears run down my cheeks, but I couldn't. That would make me even more of a target, and I wouldn't let the other kids have the satisfaction of seeing me in pain. Kids in middle school were savage. They would rather laugh at you than help or make sure you were okay. They also said the meanest and most hurtful things with no care for the impact that it had on others.

When we walked back into the classroom, I held my head high. I looked at Sarah, and she was grinning at me; I could hear the whispers around the class. I was seething; I promised myself that I wouldn't take anymore crap from her. From that day on, I would stand up for myself. She should've gotten the smacks, she should have been the one in trouble, but Sarah got away with her bullying once again. I wanted to stand up and sock her in the face, but I stayed in my seat and kept quiet for the rest of the lesson. Eventually, the bell rang, and I stood. I turned to Sarah and gave her the coldest look I could muster, and left for the cafeteria.

As I walked into the cafeteria with my head down, I bumped into somebody. I looked up and groaned again. Sarah stood in front of me, a smug look on her face that made my blood boil all over again. My usual quiet and calm nature had disappeared, and I rolled my fingers into a tight fist.

"Give me your lunch money." She said the words came out in a sneer. She stuck her hand out expectantly. Sarah towered over me, and even though I was shorter, I stood a little straighter and looked her directly in her eyes.

I crossed my arms and stared her down. "No, it's not yours."

She tried to grab it from my hand, and I pulled back, my right fist connected with her cheek, and her hands flew to her face. My reaction surprised me. I hadn't expected to hit her, but the years of bullying had built up, and I couldn't stay quiet and calm anymore. Grandma taught us not to react and that kindness was the best way to deal with horrible people. I tried, but it didn't work.

"I am sick and tired of you, Sarah. I am tired of you constantly bullying me. I am done taking your crap. Leave me alone." I yelled at her; the entire cafeteria went quiet.

Sarah was holding her cheek with both hands. There was a red welt where my fist connected with her face. The cafeteria monitor, Mr. Wells, walked over to see what all the commotion was about. "What seems to be the problem here, ladies?"

Sarah dropped her hands and looked at the floor. "Nothing, sir. I was just talking to Naomi."

I scoffed. She was not going to throw me under the bus again.

I was tired of keeping quiet every time Sarah bullied me. Mr. Wells looked at me for an answer. Most of the students knew about Sarah's reputation, but I wasn't sure if the teachers and monitors knew about it too. She was good at playing innocent and good at manipulating people until she got her way.

"She tried to take my lunch money, Mr. Wells, and I refused to give it to her," I said boldly, crossing my arms over my chest again. "When I said no, she tried to snatch it from my hand."

"Follow me, both of you. We're going to the principal's office." Mr. Wells led us out of the cafeteria, down the hall, and into the principal's office. It was the first time that I had been taken to the office due to bad behavior, but I was determined to defend myself. The anger I felt earlier was still simmering inside, and I didn't want to get into trouble because of Sarah again. I knew hitting was wrong, but I didn't think she would learn any other way.

He told us to sit and wait for the principal, Mr. Russo, to call us. Mr. Wells left, and Sarah and I sat side by side, not talking or looking at each other. A few minutes went by, and I was still angry, but I felt proud of myself for standing up to her. Maybe now other kids would too. Mr. Russo called Sarah into his office, and I placed my ear against the frosted glass wall to hear what they were saying.

"What is this I hear about you trying to take your classmate's lunch money? I thought we discussed your behavior the last time you were brought to my office, Sarah." He said sternly. "I explained that I will not tolerate this kind of behavior in my school."

Sarah stayed quiet. I couldn't see her, but I imagined her face turning beet red. I suspected that she'd been in Mr. Russo's office quite often, and from the tone of his voice, it sounded like he was tired of addressing the same type of behavior.

"Well, Sarah, do you have anything to say for yourself?" He asked. I could hear him tapping his foot on the tiled floors.

"I'll try and do better, Mr. Russo." She mumbled.

Mr. Russo sighed loudly. "This is the third time that you have been sent to my office. I have no choice but to contact your parents to discuss disciplinary measures going forward."

I heard Sarah suck in a breath. "Please don't call my parents! My father will kill me!" She pleaded. Her voice sounded panicked, and even though I'd calmed down, I felt quite satisfied that she was getting reprimanded.

"You've given me no choice, Sarah. There are consequences to your actions. You should have thought of this before you did what you did." Mr. Russo said matter-of-factly. He dialed a number on his telephone, Sarah lunged for the phone, and I could hear Mr. Russo grabbing it out of her hands. "This is no way to act, young lady! Joan, please call Mr.

Macary and tell him that I need to speak to him urgently and that he needs to pick Sarah up from school immediately." He hung up, and I could hear Sarah taking deep breaths.

"But what about Naomi? She's the one that hit me!" Sarah complained.

"Don't you worry yourself about her. She will be dealt with as well."

About 30 minutes later, an irate man burst into the office. He was tall and balding, but he looked a lot like Sarah. This must be Mr. Macary; he's scary looking.

"I need to speak to Mr. Russo about my daughter. Where is she, and what has she done now?" He shouted; the whole office went quiet.

Mr. Russo opened his office door for Mr. Macary and motioned Sarah out. "Mr. Macary, please step into my office. We have a few things that we need to discuss regarding Sarah's behavior."

Sarah sat down next to me again, and as her father walked past, he stared angrily at her. I could feel her flinch next to me, and I almost felt bad for her. I peeked at her, and there were tears running down her cheeks; she was crying silently. The door hadn't closed completely, so we could still hear most of the conversation.

"There was an encounter with another student. Sarah tried to take her lunch money. This is Sarah's third offense, and I have no choice but to give her three days of in-school suspension. We cannot tolerate this behavior, and if it continues, I will have to suspend her from school grounds."

Mr. Russo explained in a calm voice. "I have arranged for her to see the guidance counselor, but I will also need you to speak to her, please."

Mr. Macary chuckled angrily. "Oh, I'll talk to her, alright. She won't be able to sit for a week once I'm done with her."

"I don't recommend physical discipline, Mr. Macary. There are better ways to get the message across." Mr. Russo continued in his calm tone.

"Are you trying to tell me how to discipline my child? Do you feed her? Do you pay for her schooling? No? Then I suggest you stay out of it, Mr. Russo." Mr. Macary stood before Mr. Russo could respond.

The principal's door flew open, and Mr. Macary grabbed Sarah by the arm, hard enough that it would likely bruise. While he was pulling her, he was scolding her, and tears were now running freely down her face. Her face was red, and her eyes were wild with fear. I knew the feeling; Mom used a wooden spoon on our backsides when we were really naughty, and it was extremely painful. Her fear was different, though, more intense.

"I'm sorry, daddy. Please don't beat me again. I will be good!" She begged through big sobs.

Mr. Macary threw Sarah into his car and slammed the door. I had never seen Sarah so scared before, and I felt worried for her, to my surprise. As an adult, I realized why Sarah was a bully. It was no excuse, but she learned it from her father. The way he treated her was the way she treated the people around her, and it was heartbreaking.

That day, I prayed for her. I prayed that she would be safe from her father, and I prayed that she would realize that what she was doing was wrong. I prayed that she would change.

God, please keep Sarah safe...

CHAPTER 4

HOME

On my way home that afternoon after the whole thing happened at school with Sarah, I stopped at my godfather Lorenzo's house. I called him Papa, and he was one of the highlights of most days. When I could, I would stop by his house on the way home and spend some time with him. His leg had been amputated a few years ago at the knee from diabetes, and since then, he had to walk with a prosthetic leg, so I usually stopped by to see if I could help him with anything around the house.

I loved helping others.

It brought joy to my soul.

I knocked on the door and heard him shuffling on the other side.

"Who is it?" He grumbled from the TV room.

"It's me, Naomi, Papa."

I heard the shuffling again. "Hold on, child. I'm coming."

"Take your time, Papa," I shouted through the closed door.

When we found out how bad the diabetes was, we were all worried about Papa. He was upset about losing his leg for a little while, but when he got the prosthetic limb, it was like he was a new man. He said the leg worked just as well as the one that had been amputated.

After a few minutes, the door swung open, and Papa grabbed onto the door frame. He was a tall man; his head was completely bald, and his brows always seemed to be pulled together between his eyes.

"Sorry for making you wait, child. I had to get my leg on first." He smiled down at me and ruffled my hair. "How was school?"

I smoothed the flyaway hair and glared at him for messing it up. "It was good, just so much schoolwork. I hate schoolwork." Uhhhhh!

He led me inside and closed the front door. I tossed my bag at the little table that stood in the entryway. His house always felt homey. There were books lying around, his jackets hung on the hooks by the door, and a layer of dust always seemed to coat everything even though I knew he kept the house as clean as he could. It didn't bother me, though; it was cozy and warm, and it felt more like home than my own house.

"Oh well, that's all part of growing up and learning. It will help you in the long run when you must live on your own and work, just like the rest of us adults." He said," Papa flopped down onto his favorite couch. It was big, and it rocked, but the leather was starting to thin out. I'd asked him if he was going to buy a new one, and he just shook his head and rocked back and forth.

He pulled his prosthetic leg off and sighed happily as he placed the leg next to him. He sat with his eyes closed for a few moments.

"Papa, do you need me to rub your leg with liniment?" I asked while he slowly rocked. He gave a short nod, and I grabbed the bottle that held the clear brown liquid. I poured some in my hand and rubbed it on the stump of his leg. He said it helped with the pain. The prosthetic would chafe at times, so the skin was always red and angry looking.

Papa had always been so nice, especially to me. He would take me to the little boutique in town that sold the most beautiful dresses, and he would tell me to choose whatever I wanted. The dresses were made from the finest material, and they were puffy with layers of chiffon and lace. It was the only time that I felt like an actual princess. Papa would often pick me up from my house and take me shopping. Not only did I get beautiful dresses, but after he would treat me to ice cream, my favorite was the creamy chocolate with sprinkles. Those days were a few of my favorite memories, and the only time I felt like a priority or appreciated, especially when I was doing everything for Mom.

After a few hours at Papa's house, I finally made my way home. Mom wasn't home yet, which meant I had to get dinner ready. I groaned inwardly, and my shoulders slumped. If I didn't do it, I knew Mom would yell at me when she got home, and I didn't have the energy for that.

I spent a few minutes in front of the fridge, trying to figure out what to make. We had beef sausages, fresh fish, eggs, lunch meat, and a whole bunch of frozen veggies. I hated making fish; it made the whole house stink, so that was not an option. After what felt like a lifetime, I finally decided on making sautéed sausages over rice and some broccoli. The others hated broccoli, but that didn't bother me. It was the only time I could do what I wanted.

Erin was the first to come home, much to my dismay. He was tall and very talented when it came to art, but it was so unfair that Mom treated him differently from the rest of us, and Erin knew he was the favorite. Spoiled brat! He smiled at me smugly and looked over the food that I was preparing.

"What's for dinner, Naomi?" He asked, eyebrows raised at the steaming sausages. He grumbled under his breath when he looked at the broccoli.

I glared over at him. "Sausage, broccoli, and rice. Are you going to help? If not, then please leave the kitchen, Erin. I don't need any distractions."

"Nope, I don't think I feel like helping today," he said, his finger on his chin in mock thought.

"Then leave Erin; dinner will be ready in twenty-five minutes." I turned back to the pots that were bubbling on the stove. He irritated me so much that I wanted to hit him in his smug face.

"Fine, I doubt it's going to taste good anyway." He mumbled and crossed his arms.

I whipped around with the wooden spoon in my hand, my blood boiling. "Then starve, you ungrateful idiot! I don't have time for your rubbish today, so either cook for yourself or don't eat at all." I yelled at him. I knew he was egging me on, but I just couldn't help it.

"I'm telling Mom!" Erin shouted back. I took a step toward him, and he blanched.

"Go ahead, you little tattletale. See if I care." I bit back.

At 15 years old, I'd found my temper, and I couldn't seem to get a handle on it these days. I wanted to ask Mom why she treated the four of us differently, but I knew she would blow a fuse and yell at me. She might even smack me, so I didn't say anything. Marsha and Jackie were the best. They hardly ever spoke back, and they listened to me. Even though they were younger, they were the most relaxed of the siblings. Donald was the youngest of the two boys, and he drove me crazy as well, he found great pleasure in teasing me, and he would press every button he could until I snapped.

"Dinner is ready! Come and eat while the food is still hot!" I shouted so that they could all hear me, wherever they were in the house.

Once everyone had sat down, I passed out their plates. I'd ended up making sausage on white bread with mustard for Erin just so that I wouldn't have to deal with Mom shouting at me later for not catering to his every need. He was always the one that had to ask for a special order like I was his own personal chef.

"Remember that one time when you took me to the ice cream parlor, and I fell on the floor, kicking and screaming because you wouldn't buy me the ice that I wanted?" Marsha said with a big grin on her face.

"I remember; what about it?" I asked, taking a mouthful of sausage. *Not bad, Naomi.* "I also remember leaving you there on the floor, looking like you were out of your mind. And then you came running after us when you realized the tantrum wouldn't work." I looked at her with an eyebrow raised; I could feel the giggle bubbling up.

We all started laughing at the memory. Erin thought it was hilarious and forgot that he had a piece of sausage in his mouth. Suddenly the sausage lodged in his throat, and he grasped at his neck as if he could push it down with his fingers. His eyes grew large and panicked, but we had no idea what was happening.

He jumped up and ran from the house, he ran in and out of the house repetitively, and my stomach dropped when I realized he was choking. *What should I do? I can't let him die! Where are you, Mom?* I couldn't think, Erin's face was turning blue, and his fingers clutched at his throat.

Suddenly, I remembered the CPR class that I had taken and that they taught us the Heimlich maneuver. So, I ran up behind Erin and grabbed him. I placed my hands under his rib cage and told him to be still. I pumped up, and the first one did nothing.

Please, God, please save him! I pleaded, tears streaming down my face. I pumped again, and the sausage flew out of his mouth. *Thank you, God!*

I sank to the floor and pulled Erin with me. He cradled into my lap, and we sat like that for a while.

"How on earth did you manage to swallow the whole sausage? You're supposed to chew! You scared the daylights out of me!" I breathed.

"I'm never eating sausage again." Erin sobbed. "I couldn't breathe, Naomi. I thought I was going to die."

"You need to be more careful," I said while rubbing his back.

Dinner had been forgotten after Erin's choking. No one wanted to eat anymore, so I huddled everyone to the big dining table, where I sat with them to do their homework. Erin, of course, felt that he deserved to be excused from homework because he had almost died. I had no energy left to argue, so I let him be.

After homework, it was bath time. We didn't have central heating or cooling, so in summers, we had to use a fan, and in winters, we all huddled by the fire. When it got extremely cold, we would put the huge tin bath by the fire and bath right there. We lived in a three-bedroom home that was attached to my grandparents' house, the girls shared a room, and the boys shared a room. My brothers and sisters had bunk beds, and I was lucky enough to have my own twin bed. There wasn't much privacy, which I despised as I got older. I was getting the beds ready for bedtime when Donald strolled in. I groaned and huffed as he grinned mischievously at me.

"What do you want, Donald?"

"What's it like being so pale? You look like a ghost." He giggled.

"Stop it; I can tan just as well as you. I just don't go out in the sun that much." Donald had a habit of teasing me for my complexion. I'd always been extremely pale, and he knew it got to me when he did it, so he never let go of it.

"You're still pale. I think I will call you 'Whitey' from now on." He teased me.

"Donald, you're being mean, and I swear I will tell Mom when she gets home if you don't cut it out." I threatened, not that it would do anything.

"So what? Go tell her, Whitey!"

I was already angry and exhausted from today. I stormed out of the room and into his. Without thinking, I grabbed his radio and threw it out of the window. *Who's Whitey now!*

I heard a gasp behind me, and I swiped at the tears on my cheek. I hadn't even realized that I'd been crying. The teasing made me so angry. I'd always been insecure about my skin; it was almost translucent.

"I'm telling Mom you broke my radio! You threw it out the window, Naomi!" He shouted, and I felt bad for a moment.

I would face Mom; I was tired of being constantly teased. I'd had enough, and he deserved it. "Tell her, brat!"

Chapter 4

Suddenly, Donald launched himself over the bed and kicked me square in my chest. I couldn't breathe and clutched my chest. I wanted to kill him at that moment. I fell to the floor, and Donald towered over me. Even though I was older, Donald was already taller than me and weighed a lot more. I lay on the floor and tried to catch my breath. Once I felt better, I kicked off the ground and tackled him.

At that moment, Mom walked in. "What is going on?" She shouts, and I barrel down the stairs to tell her what Donald had done.

After repeating what had happened, Mom looked between us. She wasn't happy, and I expected her to take Donald's side.

If it had been Erin, there was no doubt that I would be the one in trouble. "I should spank the both of you! Donald, stop calling your sister names; you know better. And Naomi, you're the oldest; I expected more from you!"

Great, as usual, I'm the disappointment...

"There was no reason to break your brother's radio. You need to find better ways to express your anger because I won't have that in my house." She continued.

The tears started again; it was like a flood that I couldn't hold back. All the emotions and the stress from the day had me completely worked up. The words came tumbling out, and I told Mom that I was tired of being teased. I hated being so pale, and not only was I teased at school, but I had to go

43

through it at home too. I told her that I just wanted to be like everyone else so that I would be left alone.

"Child, everyone was created in God's image, but no one is alike. God doesn't make mistakes, and you should be proud of the things that make you unique. Be proud of who you are and how you were created; you are a child of God." She explained, and it was the first time in a very long time that I had heard her speak so gently and even lovingly. "Do you understand me?" "Yes, Mom." I nodded and wiped at the tears.

"As for you, Donald, if you have nothing nice to say, then don't say anything at all! You will stop this teasing, if I hear a word of it again, you will find a branch outside, and I will whack you with it. Don't try me, boy!" She said, her finger in Donald's face, and I felt a sense of power.

As we made our way upstairs, Donald stuck his tongue out at me. He pushed his fingers in his ears and made a face.

"Mom." Before I could say anything further, she turned around and saw what Donald was doing. She took the two stairs up and backhanded Donald across his face.

Donald grabbed his cheek and ran up the stairs. "Ow!" He cried, and I almost felt sorry for him, but not quite.

"You stay in your room, boy! You won't know what hit you if I hear another word from you tonight!" She shouted after him as his door slammed shut.

I made my way to my bed and kneeled before it.

"Dear God, please keep us safe as we sleep tonight. Thank you for saving Erin and for giving me the courage to stand up against that mean ole bully, Sarah, and Donald. Amen."

I stood and dusted my knees, then I climbed into bed, and sleep found me fast. The next day was peaceful, with no bullies and no drama. Nothing could prepare me for what would happen at home. I was enjoying the peace and quiet I'd had for the whole day.

I got home, and Mom was rushing around, obviously running late for something. Dinner was ready and on the table. *Thank goodness. That means I don't have to cook tonight.*

"I need to run an errand, Naomi. I'll be home later. Please get everyone bathed and in bed. I've made dinner." She pointed at the table. She was in a cranky mood. I could tell from the tone in her voice. "No company. I don't want anyone at the house, do you understand?"

I nodded and handed her the jacket. "Okay, no one in the house."

Mom rushed out the door. Once everyone got home, we sat at the table and enjoyed our dinner. The girls spoke about all the things they did during the day, and the boys were talking to each other.

After dinner, I packed the plates into the dishwasher and wiped the surfaces with a cloth. There was a knock at the door and when I opened it, our family friend, Iris, was standing there. "Hi, do you want to come out?" She asked in her quiet voice.

She'd been over quite a lot, and I enjoyed her company; she'd been one of my only friends.

"Sure, come in quick; I need to finish cleaning, and then we can go." She walked in, and before I could say anything, Mom walked in the door. She saw Iris, and I could see the anger in her eyes.

"Did I not tell you no company?" She snarled.

"Yes, but we were going to go outside. She's been around so long. I thought she was more like family, Mom." I tried to defend myself.

She stepped toward me. "She is not family." She looked at Iris. "Naomi is not coming out today, Iris. I think it's best if you go home."

At her tone, I wanted to beg Iris to stay or take me with her. Mom was unreasonably angry, and I didn't know why. I knew I'd let Iris in, but it hadn't even been five minutes.

Iris nodded and walked out. On her way, she whispered, "Sorry if I got you in trouble." And the door shut behind her.

Mom started yelling at me. It was as if she were a different person, and before long, I felt the sting of her hand against my cheek. Tears sprang to my eyes as I grabbed my cheek. She just kept yelling.

"None of you spoiled brats ever listen to me. This will not be accepted in my house!"

At that, she picked up one of Erin's plastic racetracks and proceeded to beat me with it. I tried to dodge the hits, but the racetrack connected with the back of my legs, my arms, and the final one connected with my cheek. The pain burned through me, and I screamed and cried, but she didn't stop. The beating felt like it went on forever. Eventually, she stopped, and I ran to the bathroom, locking myself inside.

I looked in the mirror and couldn't recognize the person staring back at me. The racetrack had ripped some of the skin off my cheek, and the mark was angry and red. It would become a large, raised bruise; and very noticeable tomorrow. I checked my other injuries, but luckily my clothes had prevented the marks from being too bad anywhere else on my body. I had no idea what possessed Mom, but it was the first time I had seen her like that. She's never hit me before, certainly not to that extent.

The welts were burning, and I couldn't stop the tears. The mark on my face would surely be permanent. I stayed locked up in the bathroom for hours. I tried to think about ways to cover it up for school tomorrow but realized that I would just have to make up a story instead.

The next morning, Ms. Shelton asked about the band aid on my face. She could see the bruising around it. I told her I had fallen off my bicycle and landed on my face. She looked unconvinced, and I wanted to tell her the truth, but then I would be taken away from my mom, and I wouldn't be there to take care of my siblings anymore. So, I stuck with the lie.

That had been the first time that Mom had laid hands on me, but it certainly wasn't the last.

CHAPTER 5

HIGH SCHOOL

High school was a different kind of nightmare. My body started changing, and I had no idea what was going on. Mom had never told me much about puberty, and all I really knew was what I learned from school. As I stood in front of the mirror before school, I could see the changes. My hips looked fuller, and my breasts were expanding. I dreaded the day I would need to get bras. *Oh no, I hope they don't get too big. Like Sherry, who runs track, but every time she runs, her breasts practically smack her in the face.*

Mom would start noticing too, which meant I would have to go shopping with her, and at this point, there was nothing more embarrassing. Please, God, let me have small breasts. From what we learned in class, I knew I was going through puberty. I didn't realize my body would feel so sensitive, though. My breasts hurt, and I was starting to get pimples. Not many, but a lot more than I usually had. I pulled myself together and decided to embrace the changes. It was all part of becoming a woman.

I rushed through the rest of the morning and made my way to school. Our first class was physical education, and it was the class I hated the most. Mainly because we had to get dressed in front of each other in the locker rooms, and I was shy. I remind myself that God made each of us in his image, and we were all beautiful in our own way. I'd learned to love myself a bit more since middle school.

"Alright, class, listen up." Ms. Cradle said, "We will be playing dodgeball today. Most importantly, we will do our warmup first. Stretch and take a lap around the track. When you get back, you will do four sets of lunges, leg lifts, sit-ups, and arm stretches each." She clapped her hands and looked at each of us for a moment. "Okay, let's go!"

Ms. Cradle was a tough cookie, and I was sure she forgot that she was teaching a class of girls. I wanted to remind her every now and then but chose not to in case she decided to make an example of me and give me extra exercises.

The exercise was intense, and by the time we were halfway through the sets, I was about ready to pass out. I was sure Ms. Cradle could see that, but she didn't let up. I decided to give it all that I'd got. I really wanted to play dodgeball, so passing out and missing the game wasn't an option. I pushed through and finished all the warm-up exercises.

Once the game was done, we went back to the locker rooms and the showers. I was huffing, and I knew my face was the color of a tomato. As I got undressed, I noticed a red spot inside my gym shorts, and a feeling of dread settled in my stomach. Oh no, is this what we learned about in sex ed? Not now, please, not now! I had to get to the nurse's office.

I went over to Ms. Cradle and asked her for a pass to the nurse's office.

"I'm not feeling well, Ms. Cradle."

She looked at me, concerned, but handed me the pass. "Here you go, dear. I hope you feel better."

I nodded my thanks and rushed to the nurse's office. I had no idea how to explain what I was experiencing, and I felt very embarrassed, but I was sure there were lots of girls that came in with the same thing.

"Uhm, hi. I, uh..." I started but struggled to get the words out.

The nurse looked up at me from her desk. "What's wrong, honey?" She asked as she stood.

"Uh, I think I started my menstruation." I kept my voice low and my eyes trained on the ground.

"Oh, your period?"

"Huh?" I looked up, confused.

"Are you bleeding in your private area?" The nurse said gently.

I nodded and looked back down at the floor.

"That's okay. Is this your first one?"

I nodded again, still not making eye contact. I felt color rise to my cheeks, and I wanted the floor to swallow me whole.

"Okay, I'll need to call your mother so that she knows, and then we can get you sorted here." She dialed Mom, and I listened as she explained what was going on.

When she hung up, she asked if I wanted to go home or if I wanted to finish the day at school. I decided to go home. I didn't want to feel more embarrassed than I already did, and if I was going to go through this for the first time, I wanted to be comfortable. Mom called back and asked to speak to me.

"Do you want to come home?" She asked as well.

"Yes, Mom," I said quietly.

Mom was quiet for a heartbeat. "Okay, well, the car is in for repairs, so you'll have to walk. I will meet you halfway."

The nurse gave me a sanitary pad and told me how to use it. From there, I made my way home. By the third block, I could see Mom, and we walked the last two blocks together. She didn't say anything about what was happening. She didn't offer any words of wisdom or support, and I felt completely alone. Once we got home, she left for a few minutes, and when she came back, she gave me a packet of sanitary pads and left me alone again.

What now? This feels so uncomfortable; there must be a better way to control this. I didn't know why she wouldn't talk to me about this. I thought all mothers spoke to their daughters when they got their first periods, it was like a rite of passage into womanhood, and I once again felt like I was missing out.

The pain was unbearable. It felt like something was clawing at the inside of my stomach, and I tried to ride it out, but it was just too bad.

"Mom! Where are the pain pills? My stomach hurts." I groaned and walked to my bedroom door.

She brought a glass of water and three pills and handed them to me. I spent the rest of the day in bed. The pills made me tired, and I was happy to be able to sleep through the pain. The next morning when I woke up, I found a book on my pillow. It explained why my body was going through these changes and what to expect in the future. Mom must have put it there while I was sleeping. That was probably the closest I would get to any advice.

I read the book and found the changes very interesting. It was amazing to learn how many changes a woman's body can endure and how it all worked. I felt a bit more settled at knowing what was happening to me. God is a real artist.

The one thing I was not looking forward to being was having to go through this pain every 28 days. It made me nervous, and I prayed that somehow, I would be able to go through these changes without the blood and pain, but I doubted that I would be so lucky. I had no idea how I was going to get through the semester when swimming came around; I couldn't swim with this thing on... I'd read about a thing called a tampon, but they looked terrible, and I wasn't ready for that just yet. Ugh, why do we have to go through this?

Chapter 5

The next morning, I felt so much better. It was still uncomfortable, but I could handle it. After the breakfast mania, I made it to school, and as I walked down the hallway, I noticed a cute boy looking at me. My heart rate sped up. He was around 5'7" and had a slender build with curly brown hair. He looked like he had just walked off a GQ magazine. I couldn't take my eyes off him. He had a distinguished but wild look about him, and it had me feeling flushed.

As I passed him, he stopped and looked at me again.

"Hey, can I speak to you for a second?" He asked; his smile made my breath hitch.

I looked around to make sure that he was talking to me. "Yeah, sure."

"My name's Robert. I just wanted to say you're beautiful, and I was hoping you would let me call you sometime?" He asked, magazine ready smile still in place.

"How? I haven't given you my number," I answered with a giggle.

"Oh, yes, I'm jumping ahead. Would you give me your number?" He corrected, and a blush crept onto his cheeks.

"What's your name?"

"Naomi."

"That's a beautiful name. A beautiful name for a beautiful girl." He laughed, and the sound was mesmerizing.

"Thanks." I pulled out a piece of paper and scribbled my number down on it. "Here you go." I handed him the paper, and he looked down at it for a moment.

"Thank you, Naomi. Oh, is there a specific time I can call? I don't want to annoy your parents or anything."

I smiled and tucked a piece of my hair behind my ear. "It's just my mom, and anytime is fine."

"Perfect, I'll call you soon then." With a wink, he walked away, and it took me a moment to catch my breath.

Was that real? Did that really happen? He was drop-dead gorgeous, and I couldn't wait to speak to him again. My name sounded like honey on his lips, and his deep voice made me feel warm. I had no idea what Mom would say when a boy called, but I hoped that she wouldn't mind. I also hoped that she would be excited with me, but I doubted that that would ever happen.

I felt anxious for the rest of the day, and I couldn't stop thinking about Robert and the call. By the time that I got home, I was exhausted from the nerves. At 8 PM, I heard the phone ring, and my heart skipped a beat. I stayed in my room even though I wanted to run down the stairs and grab the receiver. I listened for a few moments.

Mom answered. "Hello?" There was a minute of silence. "Naomi! It's for you!" She shouted up the stairs. I made my way down as calmly as I could. "It's Robert. Please don't talk for too long."

"Yes, Mom. Thanks." I took the phone and waited for her to disappear into the TV room. "Hello?"

"Ah, so you did give me the right number." Robert's deep voice tickled my ear.

"Huh?"

"Just joking, but I'm glad you decided to take my call. How are you?" He asked with a laugh.

"I am doing okay. I was just lying-in bed, reading a book. And you?" I said, my voice bouncing with the nerves.

"All good this side. I was just watching TV, and then I couldn't wait to hear your voice any longer."

My cheeks warmed. We spent a good couple of minutes talking about our hobbies, I told him about band and dance class, and he told me that he enjoyed music.

"I've got my next band performance in two weeks." I hesitated. "Would you, um, would you like to come?" The words rushed out.

"I'd love to. I just need to see if my mom will drop me off."

"Okay, cool. Tell me a bit more about you." I hinted. We'd spoken about me a lot, and I didn't think my cheeks could handle anymore blushing.

"Well, I am in the 11th grade, as you probably know. And I am part of the softball team. I love it; it's been a great year for us so far," he said. I could hear the excitement in his voice. "You're in the 10th grade, right?"

"Yep, I can't wait to graduate from high school and have this all be over." I sighed.

He laughed again. "Don't rush it; you might not like what's on the other side of high school. Besides, you might enjoy the last few years."

It was my turn to laugh. At least the bullying had pretty much stopped. "Yeah, you're probably right."

We spoke for a little while longer, I was completely taken by Robert, and if it weren't for Mom, I'd probably be able to talk to him for much longer. I was excited that a boy that was a year older than me liked me, and I really liked him. It all felt like a dream.

"Okay, well, I will see you at school tomorrow, Naomi. Good night, beautiful." He said."

I blushed deeply once again. "Good night, Robert." We hung up, and I just stood there for a while. My heart was beating a mile a minute, and I felt warm all over. Was he going to be my first boyfriend? The thought made me excited. For the first time, I couldn't wait for school to start. I went back to my bed and yelled to Mom that I was off the phone on my way there.

The next morning, I was awake and ready before anyone else in the house. Once I'd helped Mom get the others ready, I practically ran to school. Band class was the first of the day. While Mr. Hall went over the details for the performance, I noticed someone through the window on the door. It was Robert. A smile broke out over my face when he waved, and I waved back. I wanted to make an excuse to leave class, even for a moment but decided against it. I didn't want to come across as desperate or too interested. Mom had once said that men were more interested when you showed less interest. I'm not sure why I took her advice. She was alone and had more boyfriends than I could count. When I looked back to the window, Robert was gone, and I felt a tinge of sadness.

"Alright, class. Let's get started with our rehearsals. The show is right around the corner, and I need to know where each one of you are." Mr. Hall looked around at the class. He was one of my favorite teachers, purely because he taught band class and I loved music. "Naomi, I need you in the first chair. You'll be on the bass clarinet for today. We will go over the clarinet in our next class."

I nodded my agreement and moved to the first chair. I loved music. I loved listening to it and performing it, and it was one of the few good things in my life. And I was good at it. Grandma had been my biggest supporter, and I learned from her. She loved the clarinet as well and always pushed me to do my best.

The time flew by, and the day of the performance was here. It was Saturday, and there was a row of cars outside of Melon Hall. Parents and children were streaming in, and my palms got clammy. I was a shy girl, and sometimes stage fright got a hold of me, but I wouldn't let it ruin this for me. The excitement was almost unbearable. I wanted to show the judges that I was good, that I could be the best.

I'd hoped that Mom would be there. I just wanted her to support me, even if it was just once. She hadn't come, which didn't necessarily surprise me. I just felt the familiar sting of disappointment. Grandma came, though, and she was sitting in the front row. When I saw her, most of the disappointment disappeared. I knew she would always be there for me.

Before I knew it, it was my turn. When I walked out on stage, my heart stopped. I looked out at the audience, took my seat, closed my eyes, and breathed deeply. When I opened them again, it was just me and the blinding lights. I played my heart out, the notes from the clarinet carried out across the hall. When I was done, everyone broke out in applause. They all stood, and I couldn't breathe for a few moments, it was so amazing, and I felt like I was on top of the world.

I walked off stage and into Grandma's waiting arms. "Well done, child! That was amazing." She said into my ear.

"Thank you, Grandma. Thank you for being here." I hugged her tight again, and as I turned around, Robert was standing in the hallway just off to the side of where my grandma was sitting.

I walked over to him.

"You came?"

"Of course, I did. I told you I would, and I didn't want to miss it. You were amazing up there, a natural!" He said, and I giggled. Suddenly he pulled me into a hug, and my knees almost buckled. His arms were strong, and he smelled fresh, like mint and sandalwood. "Congrats, Naomi."

The hug ended quicker than I wanted it to, but I was so happy that he had come to watch me perform. It was one of the most magical experiences of my whole high school period. I won best in state. They gave me a huge trophy, and my face was in the town newspaper for weeks after that. It was a surreal time. And from then on, Robert and I were inseparable. I went to every one of his softball games, and he came to every practice and performance I had for music and dance.

CHAPTER 6

FLORIDA

School was finally over, and it was time for summer vacation.

I'd been waiting all year for this since I found out that I was going to Florida for two weeks. It was all that I could think about. I'd barely been able to contain my excitement. Whenever I thought of Florida, I thought of the palm tree lined streets and salt kissed ocean breeze. I thought of the beach and Universal Studios. It was pure fun in the sun and every kid's dream holiday destination. I never thought that I would have a chance to go to Florida. I never thought that I'd ever travel outside of Maryville. I would be staying with my half-brother, Sampson, and his wife, Misty.

I hadn't really known him growing up, and over the years, I'd spent a handful of times with him when they came to visit, so it was a surprise when Mom said I could go for so long. Sampson was from my father's side of the family, and I think Mom maintained contact to be polite. She helped raise him when Mom and my father started dating. They had two children, so I wouldn't be too lonely, even though they were much younger than me and Misty said she would take me out to see Florida. I was most excited to see Universal Studios, and I had been saving any money I'd made working over summers and doing chores for Grandma and Papa just so that I didn't have to ask Mom for any help.

When I heard them pull up to the house, I ran downstairs, unable to contain the excitement any longer. My bags were already packed and waiting by the door. I didn't know what to pack, so I threw in a bit of everything. Florida was known to be hot most of the time, so I made sure I had a lot of summer dresses and swimming costumes packed. Mom forbade me from wearing bikinis because it showed too much skin, and people would think I was a loose girl.

"Mom! Sampson and Misty are here!" I yelled as I got to the front door.

"Naomi, calm down for a second. I need to finish getting your snacks packed." Mom shouted from the kitchen. "Give them some time to park. They're probably tired from the drive, and they don't need all that excitement straight off the bat."

I rolled my eyes and took a deep breath. A moment later, there was a knock on the patio door. Mom wiped her hands on her apron and slid the door open. Sampson was a large man, muscles poked out from his sleeves, and he stood as tall as a giant. I'd stopped growing since the beginning of high school, so next to him, I really looked like a little girl. Misty was a little shorter than him. She looked like a model with long legs and dark skin. Her smile was bright and friendly, and I couldn't help smiling when she did.

"Hi, Estell." Sampson shook Mom's hand and motioned to Misty. "This is my beautiful wife, Misty."

"Hello, it's lovely to meet you. It's good to see you again, Sampson. Come in; you must be exhausted from the long drive!"

Mom ushered them into the lounge. "I'll get some sweet tea." "You have a lovely home, Estell," Misty said, looking around. "Oh, thank you! How was the drive?" Mom asked.

"It wasn't terrible. We left yesterday and stayed at a lovely bed and breakfast in Fayetteville just to make the trip a little easier." Sampson answered. He took a big sip from the sweet tea that Mom had handed him.

I walked in, and Misty smiled up at me, and so did Sampson. He took up most of the two-seater sofa. I felt very small compared to him, but his kind eyes made up for the intimidating size.

"Hi Sampson, Misty. I'm glad you got here safely." I said nervously.

"We're very excited to have you stay with us, sweet girl. Florida is going to be so much fun!" Misty said, her eyes sparkling.

I immediately felt comfortable around her.

"Is that an accent I hear, Misty?" Mom asked politely.

Misty giggled. "Yes, ma'am. I come from Jamaica."

"Oh, wow! I've never been. That's so interesting!" Mom gushed.

"You should visit Jamaica sometime. It's a beautiful place."

"Oh, no, no. I couldn't. I've never even left Maryland." Mom answered. She wasn't one for traveling and didn't enjoy being away from home.

"Well, if you change your mind, let me know. I can recommend some lovely places." Misty said. You could see she was passionate about her home country. I wondered what made her want to relocate to Florida.

"Thanks, but I like the good ole Florida soil. I doubt I'll change my mind." Mom sometimes came across as a bit rude when she spoke to people, and I recoiled a bit at her tone, but Misty just dipped her head in acknowledgment and looked at Sampson.

"I still love traveling. I think it's the best way to learn about the world," Sampson chimed in.

"Of course, you and your father have always been travelers. Could never quite understand it." Mom raised her eyebrows at him, and he laughed.

We sat there for about an hour just talking about their travels, what it was like in Florida, and how their children were doing. I'd never really met them, and the last time I saw Sampson was quite a few years ago, so I felt anxious, but I knew it would be a good vacation. There were so many things that I wanted to do and see. She'd given Sampson some money a little while earlier for taking care of me. I doubt it was much, and from what I heard, Sampson and Misty were well off when it came to money. I heard Mom speak about it when she'd had a few drinks and went on one of her complaining rants about my father and his family. She always made a fuss about him having so much money but never offering to help with all the children. I was sure that she would probably spend the money on alcohol and cigarettes anyway. When I had those thoughts, there were moments when I felt bad for being so bitter toward Mom. She made sure we had food and clothes and an education.

"Thank you, Estell, for your hospitality. We really must get going. It's a long drive. We will probably stay somewhere on the way again." Sampson stood and took the tea glasses to the kitchen. "We will call when we stop for the night."

I jumped up and grabbed my luggage; I was so ready to go. Sampson helped me load the luggage into the car, and I climbed into the backseat. Mom grabbed the door before I closed it. For a moment, I thought she was going to give me a hug to say goodbye. Even though I was a teenager, I still held onto the hope that she would be more loving or show any kind of affection.

"You be good now, Naomi. I don't want any news of misbehaving." Mom grunted.

"Mom, I'm sixteen years old. I know how to behave." I snapped quietly.

She didn't say anything else before pushing the door closed. A few moments later, Misty and Sampson climbed in, and we were finally on the road. The drive was good, and we stopped at a little town about halfway to Florida for the night. It was a quaint little motel, and we only had one room, but there were two double beds next to each other. I wanted to watch TV, but I fell asleep before the first commercial ended. We were on the road after breakfast the next morning, and the scenery was beautiful. It felt like everything was getting prettier the closer we got to Florida. I tried to stay awake, but eventually, I gave in to the lull of the car.

I felt a shake on my shoulder a little while later. "Wake up, sleeping beauty. We're here." Misty said in a hushed voice.

I sat up and rubbed my eyes, I'd slept for hours, and the sun was just starting to set behind a huge house. It had palm trees lining the path to the front door, and little fairy lights lit the way. The sunset made everything look romantic, and suddenly, I missed Robert. He'd left on summer vacation with his family a couple of days ago and gave me a bunch of flowers and a love letter before he'd left. I kept the letter with me and read it when I felt lonely. Even though the sun had started to creep lower on the horizon, it was still incredibly hot. The humidity was a lot stronger here than back home.

Sampson led me inside and placed my bags by the kitchen counter. The kitchen was beautiful, and so was the rest of the house. It was a modern house, and every inch of it was clean. There were decorations here and there that came from Jamaica. I remembered the colors from class. Their kids' toys were packed away neatly in little storage boxes. Despite the almost clinical cleanliness, it still felt homey and comfortable.

"Your room is upstairs, the third door to the left." Sampson motioned with his hand.

"Okay, thank you." I tried to grab my bags, but they were too heavy for me, and I stumbled over them.

"Where are my manners? Let me carry those up for you." Sampson grabbed them and led the way upstairs. "Can't let a little thing like you struggle with them."

I felt a twinge of uneasiness at that, but I figured I was tired, and it was a lot to take in on the first day. Sampson also wasn't a very warm person when he spoke. He came across as friendly but straightforward. He wasn't one for small talk.

"You'll have your own bathroom up here. The kids' rooms are upstairs as well as their shared bathroom." He opened a door that held a large bed and a vanity. There was so much space. "This is your room for the next two weeks. The bathroom is through there. Come down when you are ready."

I looked around for a few minutes. It was just as clean as the rest of the house. There were fewer personal items, but the room was beautiful. The bed was big, and the duvet looked fluffy, more comfortable, and warmer than anything I had at home. After a moment of staring happily at my new temporary home, I headed into the bathroom. I splashed my face with cool water. It was so refreshing after the long drive. I couldn't wait to take an actual shower. The shower was huge; it could fit my siblings and I in there easily. Once I was all freshened up, I made my way downstairs and found Misty in the kitchen. She was chopping something up on the cutting board in front of her.

"Hey sweet girl, are you hungry? I was just about to whip up some food." She said with a warm smile.

"Oh yes, I'd love a sandwich." Almost on cue, my stomach let out a loud grumble, and we both giggled.

"Okay, I'll make a few turkey sandwiches. We can all sit out by the pool and relax after the drive." Misty pulled ingredients out of the fridge, and I sat down by the counter.

We spoke while she made the sandwiches, and in no time, we were sitting outside together. The sun had now completely disappeared, the outside area was illuminated, but hundreds of little lights dangling from the patio ceiling. We were all tired, and I was grateful that we weren't having a big dinner. The kids were spending a few more nights with Misty's parents, and she promised that she would take me shopping the next morning.

Once I finished up my sandwich and excused myself.

The shower was calling to me. I undressed and climbed in almost robotically. Exhaustion had fully settled in now, and my arms and legs were moving on autopilot. The shower was as amazing as it looked. It was like standing in the rain, but the water was warm. Misty or Sampson had an expensive taste. The towels were unbelievably soft, and every piece of decor looked like it cost a fortune. I felt like royalty or a celebrity. I crawled into bed shortly after my shower and expected to fall asleep immediately. But I spent a lot of the time tossing and turning. I wasn't used to having a room all to myself, let alone a bed that could fit all my siblings in it.

Chapter 6

After what felt like hours, I finally drifted off into a restless sleep. At some point in the night, I was awoken by a strange noise. I opened my eyes and almost screamed when I looked straight into a dark figure standing next to my bed. I felt uncomfortable, and my heart was racing. It was Sampson. Initially, when I realized who it was, I calmed a little, but the uneasy feeling I had felt years before settled in my stomach.

I started asking what he wanted, but he placed a big, calloused hand over my mouth, preventing any sound from escaping. I squeezed my eyes shut and opened them again to make sure I wasn't dreaming. This time when I looked again, my eyes had started to adjust to the dark, and Sampson was unzipping his pants with his free hand. My stomach dropped. No, this can't be happening! He's my brother...

Everything proceeded in slow motion. He pulled his pants off and shifted his underpants. In a second, his private part was out. Disgust filled me, and at that moment, if I had the nerves and a knife, I would have cut it off. If he wanted to show it, unwarranted, then that's what he deserved. That way, this would never happen to anyone else again. I'd never seen one before, and I tried to squirm out of his grasp, but I was pinned to the bed. I felt so helpless and weak that I wanted to hit him or wriggle away, but I couldn't move. Fear had gripped me.

"Mmm," you look so sweet, Naomi, so soft and delicate." He groaned next to my ear. "I bet no man has ever touched you before." Tears rolled down my cheeks, and I tried to scream, but no sound came out. "Shh, girl. We don't want

Misty to hear. She would not be happy to see you all over her husband, would she?"

He was climbing on top of me, and I started to panic. I could feel his erection against my leg. I bit down on his hand, and he yanked it back with a yelp, more surprise than pain, but it gave me the chance that I needed. I took that moment to try and throw him off me, he was unbalanced, and it worked. He fell to the floor with a grunt, and I crawled back on the bed to the furthest point from him.

"Brat!" He hissed in a low grunt and made for the bed again.

I started kicking and tried to yell out again, but my voice was hoarse. Where was Misty? Why can't I shout? He grabbed at my feet, and I lunged at him, aiming for his eyes. "Get off of me!" I said in a soft voice, the opposite of the scream going on in my mind. I managed to scratch him, and with another curse, he ran out of the room. I wondered, no, hoped that I'd drawn blood. Maybe Misty would see the scratches and ask him what had happened. I jumped up and locked the door as soon as he was out and slid down to the floor in a heap of tears. My body was shaking uncontrollably. I wanted to leave; I wanted to go home. I'd rather be stuck in my house with Mom than be here with Sampson.

I didn't sleep for the rest of the night, afraid that he would come back and finish what he'd started. The next morning, I didn't leave my room. I kept the door locked and drifted in and out of sleep. *Why would he do this? I was still his sister.* I felt disgusted, and no amount of soap or water could take that away, and I tried. I took two showers that morning, and every time, I scrubbed until my skin was red and sensitive, but it didn't help.

I could smell Misty cooking downstairs, and my stomach curled at the thought of food. A few minutes later, I heard a knock on the door. "Food is ready, Naomi. Come down and eat." Misty's voice drifted through the closed door. She sounded like her usual friendly self, with a hint of concern, probably because it was the first proper day in Florida, and I'd been locked up in my room all morning.

I didn't want to eat. I didn't want to leave the room, but I knew that would be rude, and Grandma made sure that we had proper manners. "Okay, I'm coming!" I gathered my courage and made my way downstairs. *Maybe Misty would plan to let me go home.*

I got downstairs and sat down at the kitchen counter. I didn't look at Sampson, who was seated across from me. His gaze was burning into me. After a moment of silence, I looked at Misty. "I want to go home." "I said."

"You just got here. We still have so much to do and see! What's wrong? Are you not feeling well?" She asked; confusion pulled at her brows. She immediately made her way to where I was sitting and placed her palm against my forehead.

"I just don't feel well. I want to go home." I repeated. I didn't know why I didn't tell her what had happened the night before, but I couldn't seem to get the words out. Tears threatened to spill, and my voice wobbled.

"You're only due to go home in two weeks. We can't take you back yet. I've got work, and so does Sampson. What made you change your mind?"

I wanted to tell her so badly. I looked over at Sampson. I'd managed not to make eye contact the whole time, but at that moment, the intensity of his stare was palpable. The look he gave me told me that if I said anything, there would be major consequences. So, I bit my tongue. I didn't know him; I had no idea what he was capable of, and I didn't want to find out either.

"Why don't I take you for a drive? We can get some ice cream." Sampson said, the predatory look still in his gaze. "We can drive to Universal Studios and buy tickets for the weekend."

"No... Thank you," I said a little too quickly. "I think I've come down with a stomach problem. I'd rather just eat and go back to bed if that's okay?"

They looked at each other, and after a moment, they nodded. I finished my food in silence and went back to my room. I locked the door and sat by the window. My first trip to Florida and it was ruined on the first night. I hadn't even been there a full day. The anger bubbled up, and I wanted to break everything. I wanted to throw things and tear things, but I just sat there silently. I felt betrayed.

I spent the rest of the holiday watching my every move. Misty took me out a few times to do shopping and go to the beach. I managed to keep my distance from Sampson, but I felt him watching me, I felt him follow me around, and I felt him lurk in the hallway at night. I'd seen a shadow from under my door a few times since the first night, and I stared at it without moving until it eventually disappeared. I cried most nights, and during the day, I stayed in my room unless Misty took me out. She asked a lot of questions and tried to cheer me up, but it didn't work. I enjoyed the times that we went out and did girly things, things that girls at school usually did with their moms, like getting their hair and nails done or buying clothes. It was nice until we got back to the house.

After what felt like forever, the two weeks were finally over, and we made our way home. Everything was a lot duller on the way back, I didn't bother taking in the scenery, and I fell asleep almost immediately when the car moved. When we got home, I gave Misty a hug and greeted Mom. The moment the pleasantries were done, I ran upstairs and closed my door. I knew Mom would scold me later for running off before they were gone, but I couldn't stand being in Sampson's company a moment longer.

I didn't want to see Sampson ever again. It was the second time I felt pure hate in my short life, hate that someone stole a part of my innocence. Hate that it was someone I knew, and it was someone that was meant to take care of me. Why did these men think it was okay? I couldn't understand it, and I wished that at some point, they would understand what impact their actions had on my life. I just hoped that neither of them tried to do these things with other girls. I prayed that night when I got home, I prayed that God would show them the error in their actions, and if that didn't work, I prayed that God would keep any other girls safe that encountered them. Prison should be their portion.

CHAPTER 7

MOVING OUT

The end of high school finally arrived; I was excited to be done with it. The next big step was college. I wanted to study law, I wanted to help women and children that had similar experiences to mine, and as I grew older, I started to realize how often it happened. After a lot of the day-to-day experiences that I had and a few of them that I had witnessed, my heart was set on defending the innocent. I worked hard during holidays and weekends throughout middle school and high school. Babysitting in middle school was my regular job. I managed to babysit on weekends and on the odd weeknight when I finished helping with my siblings. High school offered an opportunity to work more. My siblings were getting older, and they could take care of themselves, so I started working as a server at a local ice cream parlor over the weekends and at a restaurant on some weeknights and every evening on weekends. I was determined to pay my own way. Mom didn't think we needed college. She wanted each of us to jump into a mediocre paying job as soon as we were finished with school.

It took a long time to build up the money; it was tough to keep it from Mom too. I knew if she found out that I even had a savings account, she would make sure that I give it to her for 'safekeeping,' and I would never see that money again. Every time I went to work, I gave her a portion of it and told her that it was all that I earned. She believed me for the most part. Over the years, I managed to save a good portion of my college fees; the rest I'd have to make up while studying.

The time came, and after a lot of arguing and being blamed by Mom for abandoning her and my siblings, I left for college. I was so happy to finally get out of the house, away from Mom and raising my siblings. It was a nerve-wracking journey, but once I'd arrived and gotten into the hang of things, college was amazing. I barely slept so that I could work and make sure I made good grades. It was exhausting, but at the same time, it was very rewarding. In my final year, I had to work with lawyers, we were given a few choices of who we wanted to work with, and I chose someone that was in a similar field to what I wanted to work in. I graduated in the top five of my class and started applying for work.

Robert had been my only happiness during the last part of high school, and we were still together during college. I loved him, and we wanted a life together. After a year, we did just that. I found out that I was pregnant with my first baby, and we were both very excited to welcome our baby boy into the world. I was determined to be the best mother I could be;

I would be better than Mom. My journey into law fell onto the back burner for a while. I put all of my efforts into being a mom and making sure that I could give our boy, Ricky, the best life that I could.

Shortly after becoming a mother, a part of my world came crashing down. Robert and I had reached a point in our relationship where we weren't moving forward anymore. We weren't growing together, and things had become stagnant.

He was a loving father and a good partner, but the relationship wasn't beneficial to either of us, so we decided to go our separate ways. Robert remained a constant in Ricky's life, and he was always willing to help where he could. Being apart was better, and not only were things amicable, but we stayed friends, which made a big difference in how we raised Ricky. There were times when I missed him and being with him, but I knew it was mostly loneliness speaking.

After the break-up, which wasn't toxic or bad at all, I had to move into an apartment with Mom. I went through a stage where I was struggling to stay afloat as a single mom, so I had no other choice. I managed to find my first proper job with a bigname company; I helped with paperwork and learned how to work in a corporate space. The pay was enough to get by, and I worked to a point where I was able to spoil Ricky every now and then. It was an unfair battle with Mom, though, because I had to pay for most of the household things like food and utilities, whereas Mom only paid half of her rent. It didn't surprise me that I would, once again, have to pick up the slack, but it meant that most of my earnings went to surviving.

The first few months went relatively well. Mom and I kept to ourselves and lived past each other. She didn't really want anything to do with Ricky and mentioned a few times that she wasn't interested in being a grandmother. It was sad because Ricky wanted her attention, especially since we all lived together, but she wouldn't blink an eye in his direction. He was just entering his toddler years, so he couldn't understand why his grandmother didn't want to hold him, talk to him, or play with him. It was frustrating, and it was at those times that I wished that I had a better mother. The only consolation was that when Ricky spent a weekend with Robert, I knew his parents made sure to spoil Ricky. They spent a lot of time together, and Robert often sent photos and videos of them playing. Despite the lack of attention from Mom, Ricky was growing into a loving young man.

Mom had a steady stream of boyfriends over the years. I'd told her not to bring them into our apartment for Ricky's safety, so she would be out most of the time. Eventually, because of all the nights out and the drinking, she stopped paying her portion of the rent. She didn't speak to me about it or ask if I was able to cover her half; she just stopped. I couldn't pay for the full rent and still keep us afloat, but when I confronted her about it, she would snap at me or wave me off and disappear again for days on end. I was facing major strain, and my performance at work was dropping because of the stress at home. Ricky started spending more time with Robert, which made me feel like a terrible mom, but I didn't want him to suffer with me. I tried to speak to my siblings about either taking Mom in or helping financially, but they all said no. I tried to maintain a relationship with them over the years, but we barely spoke. Erin didn't respond to any messages or calls. According to Grandma, he moved to a different city and didn't speak to her either. Donald and I never got along, even after high school, so I didn't speak to him at all. And as for my sisters, we messaged every few weeks, but they were the general pleasantries. I wasn't even sure where they were or what they were doing except that Marsha had gotten married right out of high school to someone much older. I was happy for them; I wanted them to have good lives. After playing such a major role in raising them, I just wished they would have included me in their lives. Ricky had never met any of his aunties or uncles. After asking them to help with Mom, I realized I was on my own. Jackie, unfortunately, followed in Mom's footsteps. After she dropped out of high school, she started drinking, and before long, she was a full-blown alcoholic. I didn't want to give up on her, though. She was an intelligent woman, and letting her ruin her life over alcohol wasn't an option, so I planned an intervention. It happened about a month ago. I knew where her usual pubs and liquor stores were. One afternoon, I parked outside the store and watched as Jackie stumbled out holding a brown bag covering a bottle of alcohol that was already open. She hadn't expected to see me, and even though it was 11 AM, she was already drunk. Once I called her over, she climbed into my car. I'd packed a bag for her, and after a very serious conversation and describing what her life would be like if she continued the way she was, she agreed to go to rehab. I dropped her off, and she stayed for a few months. She was sober when I picked her up again, and I prayed that she would continue on in that way.

Mom was becoming increasingly abusive at home. It was mostly verbal abuse, but on occasion, she would pinch me or hit me if she was really drunk. The last and the worst attack happened almost one year into living in the apartment together. That night, Mom was drunk again. She'd been out with a guy and stumbled through the door around 10 PM. I had just put Ricky to bed, and I was cleaning the kitchen when she stumbled past me, almost dropping her beer bottle. I shook my head and sighed.

"What's your problem?" She mumbled.

"Nothing, Mom. You're drunk, again, and I don't want to talk about it."

"Oh good, I don't want to hear about it anyway." Mom stumbled backward and leaned against the kitchen wall.

"You need to pay your rent money this month. I can't cover it," I said and returned to the dishes in the sink.

"Well, I don't have the money, so you're just going to have to make a plan, aren't you?" She took a swig from her beer and burped. "You have that fancy job, those fancy clothes, and that boy of yours goes to a fancy school. You're not broke; you're just being selfish as usual." Another burp.

"No, Mom. I don't have any more money left. I told you last month was the last time that I would be able to help." I put the glass I was washing down in the sink and held onto the side of the counter, an effort to control the emotions that were threatening to spill. "Maybe if you stopped drinking and going out so much, you'd have enough money to cover your responsibilities." I barely got the last word out when I felt a crack against my head.

Everything went blurry for a second, and when I stepped back, there was a sharp pain in my foot. I bent down and pulled a piece of blood-covered glass from my heel. There were pieces of glass all around me, and it took a few moments to realize what she had done. I could feel something warm trickle down the back of my head through my hair.

"What the heck, Mom!" I groaned. I wanted to use a stronger curse word but stopped myself before it tumbled out. She'd hit me over the head with her beer bottle. *A beer bottle!* I hardly ever swore, but anger was rising through the dizziness.

Mom surged forward and rammed her knee in my stomach while I was still bent over. I collapsed on the floor from the impact. Seconds later, her hand was tangled in my hair, and she started pulling me across the kitchen to the bedroom. Glass scratched my bare arms and legs, but I couldn't feel anything except the pain in my head. I underestimated her strength.

"You foul little girl! How dare you speak to me like that. You think you're old enough to question me?" She stumbled over the words as I kicked and thrashed in her grip. She eventually stopped by my bedroom door. Ricky was asleep on the other side, and I prayed that he wouldn't wake up. Mom grabbed my face with her thin, boney fingers. "Question me again, and I'll kick you and that little runt out on the streets."

Her face was so close to mine. I could almost taste the stale beer on her breath. I wanted to point out that since I was paying for the apartment, I could kick her out on her butt, but Ricky's safety was more important. I didn't know what she would do to him if I fought back or threatened her. She squeezed my cheeks hard enough to bruise and then let go. After the last sneer, Mom spat on the floor where I was still lying in shock and stalked off into the kitchen. I could hear her rummaging through the fridge, *probably for another beer*. I slipped into the bedroom and locked the door. The back of my head was still bleeding where she had hit me, and my ribs ached. Luckily, once I'd cleaned it up and determined that it was serious enough for stitches, I made sure there would be no injuries for Ricky to see. I looked over at him. He looked so peaceful as he slept, completely unaffected by everything that happened. Relief washed over me that he hadn't woken up from all the commotion.

I can't live like this anymore. I need to get my baby out of here. I spent the rest of the night crying and trying to figure out how to get him to a safer environment. Eventually, two short hours before sunrise, exhaustion pulled me under. I fell asleep holding Ricky as close as I could without waking him. The house had become so toxic that Mom and I had no relationship at all, and eventually, it would have more of an effect on Ricky. As soon as the sun came up, I packed our bags and as much of our things as possible and had it ready for us to leave. I'd decided that I would leave after work the next day, Mom was already gone, and by the looks of it, she would be away for a day or two, so I didn't have to worry about running into her. I cleaned the glass and drops of blood in the kitchen before getting my happy boy ready for daycare. I packed all of our things into my car, as much as I could fit in, along with any valuables, and took one last look at the apartment as we left. Ricky and I would survive even if I had to ask Robert for help. *This will never happen to you. I will never allow anyone to harm you.*

Once I got to work, I asked my manager if I could leave early due to a personal situation. For once, he was in a giving mood and allowed me to leave. The last thing, and probably the most important, was to find a place to sleep. I spent most of the afternoon thinking of who I could call and who would be willing to help.

After a few minutes of staring at my cell phone, I took a deep breath and decided to take a chance. The phone rang three times.

I was about to hang up when the line clicked.

"Hello?"

"Theresa? Hi, it's Naomi. I have a major favor to ask." I said hesitantly.

Theresa had been my roommate in college and one of my closest friends. After college, we became best friends, and even though life kept us from seeing each other regularly, we spoke almost every day. She had just moved into a new development; we'd celebrated with a bottle of champagne on her owning her own house—she was my only hope. Otherwise, I'd have to find a homeless shelter for a few nights, and I didn't want to put Ricky through that. He was already confused by the packed car this morning. Theresa knew about my mom, and she'd offered for us to move in when she bought the house, but I didn't want to be a burden back then. Now I'd have to bite back my pride and ask. I told her what had happened the previous night, and she stayed silent for a while.

"Is that invitation for a room still open? I promise I can pay rent and buy food and whatever else we need. Ricky won't be a burden; you won't even notice that we're there. Please, T, even if it's just for a little while." I was on the verge of begging; my nails were bitten down to the beds, and I was sure I'd have bruises on my palms from clutching the phone so hard.

I couldn't stomach staying with Mom, the abuse had gone on too long, and Ricky deserved so much more than a grandmother that didn't love him. My grandma adored him, and so did Papa, but they were getting old and wouldn't be able to take care of me and Ricky. Besides, if I moved to either of them, Mom would know where we were, which defeated the purpose of getting away from her abuse. She didn't know Theresa; she didn't bother getting to know anyone in my life, so it was the safer choice. The only thing better than living with someone she didn't know would be to live in a different town, but that wasn't an option at that moment.

"Girl, you know you two are welcome anytime. I'll clear the spare room this afternoon. Don't worry about furniture or any of those things; I've got that sorted. We can talk about rent and stuff once you two are settled." Concern and love filled her voice.

My heart felt like it wanted to beat out of my chest and stop all at the same time. "Thank you, T. You have no idea how much this means!" I gushed; tears streamed down my cheeks. I didn't realize how stressed I was about this until now. We hung up, and I sobbed in my car. Once I managed to pull myself together, I went to the store, bought our favorite bottle of champagne and a few other things to contribute to dinner, and made my way to pick Ricky up. When Ricky hobbled excitedly out of daycare like he did everyday, I scooped him up in a massive bear hug, and the tears from earlier threatened to spill again. I kissed his forehead and breathed deeply.

"We're going to visit Aunty T for a while. Okay, baby?" I kissed him on his little head.

"T, T, T!" He chanted, he couldn't speak yet, but he'd always loved being around Theresa. She spoiled him and showered him in love whenever we visited, so I knew this would be a good adjustment for both of us.

Theresa was waiting for us as we got there, Ricky hobbled over to her, and she wrapped him in a big hug before helping me with our bags. Home. Maybe this would be home. I dared think for a second that my luck was turning around.

What a silly thought...

CHAPTER 8

THERESA

Life was, dare I say, good. Theresa and I went right back to our roommate days, minus the parties and with a few more responsibilities. We took turns cooking and doing all the normal domestic things and often enjoyed a glass of wine together after dinner. Ricky adjusted incredibly, and he was flourishing now that he received so much love and attention, and he wasn't being ignored or pushed away. Theresa was the aunt he never had. The house was big compared to what I grew up in and the apartment we stayed in with Mom. I was able to buy a little bed for Ricky, and even though he still slept by me most nights, he often fell asleep in his own bed that I'd pushed next to mine, and when he woke up during the night, he would crawl in next to me and cuddle up as close as he could. We were happy and comfortable in our new home.

I hadn't heard from Mom in weeks, besides a scathing message shortly after we left. I'd read the first sentence, which was a string of cuss words and accusations of being a selfish girl and no daughter of hers. After that, I deleted the message and blocked her number; that was the only way to actually be rid of her. I'd told Grandma what had happened and asked her not to tell Mom where I was. She was disgusted at her behavior, but no one was surprised. Mom's downhill spiral had started years ago. I'd always suspected that Mom never wanted children. Why she had five was beyond me. I often thought back to when I was a child and, on the rare occasion that I could visit a friend, how different it was to see a normal family. Our normal was nothing like theirs, and I envied it. As an adult, I accepted the fact that Mom was just a manipulative narcissist, and she would never change. She didn't think she was wrong, and unless some miracle happened to change her mind, she would just continue the path that she had chosen. Sometimes it was better to cut toxic people out, even if they were family. Once I'd decided to cut her off, and we'd moved in with Theresa, life was so much better.

One afternoon, I had a day off from work, and I made the most of it by doing as little as possible at home. I watched my favorite TV shows and even read most of a book that I'd wanted to read for the longest time. It was a self-help book that gave you guidance on how to change your life by being positive and keeping your faith strong. I made notes and set goals as I read.

Theresa had come home early but left shortly after to run a few errands with the promise of sharing a bottle of wine when she returned. Ricky was spending the night with Grandma, so it was the first night without him in weeks. I forgot how much you miss your child when they aren't home. Robert and his wife had moved to a nearby town, so he saw Ricky a little less, but he made sure to help where he could. I settled on the sofa again and turned some music on to make the silence manageable.

A few moments after Theresa left, there was a knock at the door. It was her older brother. I'd only met him a handful of times while we were in college and once or twice since moving into the house. He was friendly and sweet, but I didn't really know him well since they weren't exactly close. He was the typical jock back in college, tall and all muscle with the boyish good looks that he knew how to use to his advantage, and since he was a few years older, he avoided us like the plague back then. It wasn't cool to hang out with your baby sister and her friends in college. The few times he'd visited the house was to borrow Theresa's car or to sleep on the couch after a night of partying. It seemed like he never really grew out of the college phase.

"Brock, what are you doing here?" The smell of alcohol hit me like a wave, and I felt nauseous as it brought back memories of Mom and her drunken escapades at home.

"T, where's T?" He slurred over his words.

"She's out running errands; she'll be back soon, though," I said, not moving out of the way.

He tilted his head as he looked at me. "She said I could chill here for a little while. Said you'd let me in." He smiled charmingly, or what was his attempt at charm.

I bit my lip, I felt anxious, but that was silly. *It's just Theresa's brother*, I chided myself internally. *It was just your stepbrother too...* The dark little voice in my mind answered as I stepped aside to let him in. The hair on my neck stood up at the memory, and I shook myself, trying to get rid of the images that rushed back.

"Okay, well, you know where everything is. You can watch TV or whatever until T gets back." I said over my shoulder and made my way toward my room. "There are snacks in the cupboard, and I think T put a few beers in the fridge."

He closed the door, and then there was silence. The uncomfortable feeling peaked as I got to my door. I turned in my doorway and jumped to find Brock right behind me. The smell of whiskey and beer made me want to gag. He must've been drinking for a few hours for the smell to be so strong. He was standing close enough for me to feel the heat radiate from his body. I took a step back into my bedroom and put a hand on my door, realization dawned that I was alone at home, and I didn't think our neighbors would hear if I screamed.

"What do you want, Brock? The TV is on. You know how everything works."

"You know, you've always been the sexiest of my sister's friends. With that perky little butt and gorgeous legs." His gaze ran up and down my body. Chills crept up my neck. "You were with that Richard guy back then, right? But word on the street is that you're single."

"Robert." I corrected; the words took a minute to sink in. I ignored the comment on my relationship status and tried to close my door, but he put a large palm against it.

"Aww, come on, sexy. You know you'd enjoy it. Admit it; you've thought of me naked before. Touching you." He stumbled over his words. What was meant to sound seductive came out as more of a mumble and a hiccup.

I struggled against the door. "No, Brock, listen to yourself. You sound like a foolish man! I don't think of you like that, and I never have. You're drunk. Walk away, and we can forget about this." I tried to reason with him, tried to keep the panic at bay, and pushed on the door again.

He hiccupped again. He was a solid weight, and the door wouldn't budge. "No, I think I might indulge myself. You'll enjoy it, I promise. I always make sure my woman enjoys it."

Bile went up in my throat at the hunger in his drunken eyes. He was going to take what he wanted, and I wouldn't be able to stop him. He was more than double my size, and I was using most of my strength trying to close the door while he barely used any to hold it open. The only advantage I had was that he was drunk, and if I timed it correctly, I could mess up his balance or something and get the door closed. That was if he didn't try to bash the door down once it was locked. He seemed like the type that wouldn't stop until he got what he wanted.

Brock tried to move into my room, but he stumbled on the threshold. I took my chance and rammed my shoulder into the door with all the strength I could muster. He grunted in surprise and stumbled backward. I pushed again, and this time, the door slammed shut on his fingers. He yelped as blood colored my cream door and carpet, the door had closed on the tips, and they'd burst from the force of the door slamming. He snatched his hand back, and I quickly locked my door. I slid to the floor, breathing hard as the panic and relief took over. Silence, I didn't hear footsteps. I couldn't hear anything above the blood pounding in my ears. Minutes passed, and I thought that he'd left, but then there was a huge bang, and the door rattled on the hinges. A squeak escaped from my lips, and I held my hand over my mouth.

"You're missing out, Naomi. I would've made you scream." He grunted through the door.

I wanted to laugh at his ridiculous statement. "Never in a million years would I desire a man like you. You make my skin crawl…." I said under my breath. I wanted to yell it at him, but I didn't want to make him angry. He could easily knock my door down if he tried.

Moments later, I listened as he shuffled away. I didn't dare open the door in case he came back, but my heart steadied when I heard the front door slam. *Why on earth did he come here?* Maybe he wanted to see Theresa, but in his drunken state, when he came home and found me alone, he'd changed his mind. I wasn't sure, but I didn't want to dwell on it either. I was just relieved that he was gone.

I took a few steadying breaths; I was starting to despise men. I'd had more bad experiences with them than good, and I was getting tired of it. I spent a few minutes gathering myself and wiping the tears that painted my cheeks. I didn't want to tell Theresa. There was no point in causing drama between them. I'd handled it myself, just like I did every other situation. I just want someone else to take care of me for once. *I just want someone not to hurt me for once*. I stayed there until I heard the front door again. I didn't move until Theresa called out for me. We made dinner, and Theresa chatted animatedly while I stayed quiet, except for a few comments and questions here and there.

The rest of the evening was soured for me. I tried to enjoy the time with Theresa, but I couldn't get the afternoon out of my head. We drank wine, and Theresa made small talk. After the second tear-jerking romance movie, I called it a night and retreated to my room. I tried to convince myself that things would get better. I would find the love I deserved, even if I had to learn to love myself. And if it ended up being just Ricky and myself, I'd be happy with that too. I wouldn't let these bad experiences change who I was, and I would try not to let them sour my opinion of men in general. It was unfair of me to say that they were all bad just because I'd happened to come across a handful of horrible ones. I prayed and thought of the book I'd read earlier. I would allow myself that evening to be upset, but I would be positive the next day.

A year later, we were at one of Theresa's family gatherings. I was helping with the food while Ricky played with a few of the other children that were there. It was the first time I saw Brock since that day at the house. He didn't pay any attention to me; he didn't even look in my direction. He was walking with a cane and speaking to a few of the older men in the family. Theresa told me that he'd stopped drinking after he had an accident on his motorcycle after a night of partying. Anger surged through me at the fact that he had created so much fear in me, and he couldn't even look at me. He probably didn't even remember that day while it took a long time for me to move on from it. I wanted to take the cane and hit him over the head with it. I smiled at the image in my mind. *Dirty bastard. I hope that whatever injury you sustained was a painful one.* Even through the anger, there was a low satisfaction that he had to walk with a cane, that somehow big ole Brock had been made smaller by an accident while being drunk. Despite the emotions running through my mind, a small part of me was glad that he'd managed to stop drinking before it consumed his life. Some traumas are learning experiences; they can help you relate and talk to others that experience the same things.

Shortly after the gathering, I managed to land a new job. The pay was better, and I had a lot more responsibility within the company. The only downside was that my car had broken down a week before, so I had to walk to Grandma's house with Ricky so that she could drop me off at work and then take him to school. The self-care took a knock on the lack of independence, and I had to remind myself not to be too critical and that I was working hard to build myself up again. The words I'd taken up and kept repeating were that a bad day was just that; it wasn't a bad life. Even though there were bad days, I tried not to complain. Every day above ground was a good day, and I wanted to embrace being alive. *This, too, shall pass.* I wouldn't give up or allow the sadness and hopelessness to consume me.

In addition to my normal work, I'd taken up a weekend job at the local hospital. I wanted to help people, and it was the best way that I could, even though it was only temporary. I assisted the nurses and kept the patients' spirits up. It made me feel like I was making a difference as well. I spent most days in the children's ward when I wasn't needed elsewhere and read books for the kids; they delighted in the funny stories. It took their minds off of whatever pain or illness they were experiencing at the time, and it also reminded me that there was still good in the world. Sometimes I would let Ricky come with me. He loved bringing his toys and sharing them with the kids. He was a social kid, and he was amazing at interacting with the children. He was a natural, and they just loved him.

Winter was the toughest time. Having to walk with Ricky to Grandma's house was painfully cold, and I made a point of bundling him up in as many jackets as I could. One particularly chilly morning, it was raining, and the wind was howling, sending an icy chill through any opening in our clothes. Ricky was shivering as we made our way to the house, and I tried to cover him from the wind as much as I could with our umbrella, but even that was straining against the force. Just as it became almost unbearable, a city bus for the handicapped stopped next to us. The driver, an old man with grey hair and wrinkled skin, poked his head out of the window, taking our shivering bodies in for a moment.

"Where are you two headed, miss?" He asked. Concern pulled at his brows.

"Four blocks down that way, sir." I pointed in the direction that we were walking.

"Why don't you two jump in? I'll drop you off as close as I can. You and your little boy can't walk in this cold." He opened the door to the bus. "This winter is a brutal one; snow is on its way. You'll catch your death out here."

"Are you sure? I don't have any money to pay...."

"No need, miss. It's on my way. I wouldn't be able to live with myself if I left you two to walk. It's the coldest it's been in years, and your boy must be chilled to the bone," he said warmly. He rubbed his gloved hands together.

"Thank you." I ushered Ricky into the bus, and we both sighed at the warmth that enveloped us.

I was always nervous when it came to men. Against my efforts to be more trusting, I always expected the worst, and I found myself surprised when he simply did as he said and dropped us off right by Grandma's house. His kind gesture warmed me; I was reminded that maybe not everyone was bad. Maybe there were more kind people out there. He was a complete stranger. He could have driven past, like so many others had that morning, but I felt like he was a blessing. Not just from saving us from the cold but also restoring some of the trust I had lost. I was sure that he thought he was just helping two cold people, but it meant so much more to me. The cold was forgotten on the short ride as Ricky chatted excitedly with the old man.

My only regret was that I hadn't asked for his name. As I got older, I thought about the gesture often, and I wanted to thank him again. I decided I would pay the kindness forward. I'd help wherever I could, and I would make a concerted effort not to judge others based on my past experiences. God created us to love and help one another, and I often lost sight of that. The bus driver was a reminder.

CHAPTER 9

DOWN ON LUCK

Moving on your own is tough. After living with Theresa for over two years and building my way up the corporate ladder, I'd finally managed to save enough money to move myself and Ricky into our own home. It wasn't anything fancy or big, but it was our own space, and Ricky even had his own room. The weekend of the move, I left Ricky with Robert so that I could unpack the boxes and get the place feeling like home before Ricky came back. Theresa and her boyfriend, Grant, helped with the heavy things, which made life a lot easier. There were many tears, happy and sad that we weren't going to be living together anymore, but they were moving toward settling down together, and despite Theresa's objections to Ricky and me being in the way of that, I knew it was time to move forward and let them start their lives together in their own home.

By the time we were done, I was exhausted. Walls of boxes crowded every room in the house. After a celebratory glass of champagne, Theresa and Grant left. It was the first weekend that I would be completely alone in my own apartment. It was a lonely but invigorating feeling. I felt like I'd finally accomplished something big on my own. The neighborhood was great, it was safe, and we had a playground close to the house. Ricky's school was walking distance away, which ultimately sealed the deal for me. Theresa and Grandma also lived a short drive away, so it was a good location. I spent the weekend unpacking box after box until there were only a few things left. My favorite part of moving was being able to decorate the way I wanted to.

Ricky was so excited when Robert dropped him off. When I opened the door to his bedroom, he just stared for a moment. He looked up at me and then back at the room. I'd decorated it with his favorite things. In the corner was a reading nook and a beanbag, his duvet had his favorite superheroes on it, and toy boxes lined the wall. It was a proper little boy's room, and it was his. Grandma and Theresa bought a few more toys as a welcoming gift for Ricky, and I left his favorite stuffed bear on his pillow.

"It's yours, Ricky." I nudged him forward, and at the touch, he came alive.

Ricky jumped on the race car-shaped bed and rummaged through the toy boxes. It was the happiest I had ever seen him, and my heart warmed. That night while he slept in his new room, I cried tears of relief and joy that I was finally able to give him more, to give him a better life. We still had a long road, but we were making progress.

The week after the move, Grandma helped me buy a car. She took me to the local dealership, and after an hour or so, I managed to secure a small car. Nothing fancy, it was something to get us back to being independent, and I wouldn't have to rely on Grandma or Papa for lifts to school and work. Peace, I felt peace. After not knowing what the future would hold, I finally felt like I was finding my feet. It was a bittersweet moment. This time I made sure to take insurance on the apartment and the car so that if anything bad happened, I'd be covered. Ricky loved driving around in the car, we even took Grandma and Papa out for ice cream or shopping, and they loved it too. I was able to take him to visit Robert more often; we made snacks for the trip and played games in the car like I *Spy* and *The Singing Game*.

One evening, I pulled up to my apartment after work. Ricky was with Grandma, and I had to pick him up. I was delayed with work, so she picked him up from school. I had to make a stop at home first to get a few books for Grandma before heading over to her house. The sun had already set, and the nighttime shadows were creeping in. *I need to get lights for the pathway.* I made it to my door when I heard footsteps around the corner. Panic swelled as a large hulking man appeared. I couldn't make out his features properly because he was wearing a black hoodie and jeans. His body language made me immediately realize that this was not a friendly visit. Before I could say anything, the man pulled a knife out of his pocket and held it to my neck. I held my hands up to show that I wasn't a threat. My heart was beating out of my chest, and my palms felt clammy in the cool night breeze. *No, no, no. I don't have time for this.*

"I don't have anything for you. I don't carry money or anything of value." I tried to reason, my voice shaking from the panic. I was so tired of all the bad things that constantly seemed to happen as soon as life started looking good.

Anger seemed to emanate from him at my words. He tilted his head which allowed me to get a look at his face. He was younger than I expected, around my age. His face was clean, the only mark was a small scar, and a shadow of stubble lined his jaw. He looked like your average neighbor, but his brown eyes were wild and unfocused.

I was relieved that I had stuffed my apartment keys into the back pocket of my jeans because the next moment, the man snatched the purse from my hand and ran into the back of my house, which was on the edge of a wooded area. I unlocked my door and ran inside, slamming it behind me. I took a few moments to breathe and thank God that I wasn't hurt or that Ricky wasn't with me. I called Theresa and explained what had happened. I knew my words were a jumble and probably didn't make much sense. I was worried that the man would return, I turned all of my outside lights on, but I couldn't see anything.

"Slow down. Are you okay? Is Ricky with you?"

Chapter 9

"No, he's with Grandma. The guy just ran away." I said, tears jumping to my eyes. My whole body was shaking from anger and fear.

I could hear Grant say something in the background, and there was a whole lot of movement. A second later, he shouted that they were on their way. I sat on the floor by the front door after giving Grandma a call to let her know what had happened and that I would be late. She was concerned but told me not to worry about Ricky and that I was welcome to sleep there as well, but I declined. I didn't want to impose, and since Ricky would be safe there, I preferred to sleep at home to make sure that the guy didn't come back. I'd worked so hard to make this house a home, and even though I had insurance, I didn't want to leave it unguarded. I couldn't afford to start from scratch all over again.

Theresa and Grant arrived, they brought a few of Grant's friends with them, and they looked extremely intimidating. There were four of them in total, large and holding handguns. Without a word, I pointed in the direction that the man had run in, and they left to look for him. During the time that they were searching for him, I called the local police station to make a report, and all the while, I was praying that the guys would find him so that the police could take him in and I wouldn't have to worry about him coming back. After about an hour of searching, they came back. Grant shook his head at my hopeful expression. They hadn't found him. Seconds later, red and blue lights flashed a short distance away. The police arrived and did another check. They took my report, and shortly after they left, a detective arrived. He sat me down in my dining room and showed me many photos of criminals who were active in the area that had been arrested before.

"Try and think of any distinguishing features, ma'am. These guys change their appearance often, so he may not look the same. But if you can remember his eyes or the shape of his nose or any scars, then we may be able to identify him." He was friendly and genuinely concerned, which made me hopeful that they would do all they could to find the man.

I looked at each of the photos for a long time, the men all looked different, but one of them stood out. I pointed him out once I was sure that it was the same guy, he'd shaved his beard since the photo had been taken, but he also had a small scar above his right eye, identical to the man in the photo, along with the same color of hair and build. And those eyes, I would never be able to forget the wild, desperate look in them. I knew if I had tried to defend myself or said something wrong, he would have used that knife. I was certain I would have nightmares for weeks to come.

"That's him."

"Are you sure, ma'am?" The detective asked.

I nodded. "Yes, his beard is shaved, but he has the same body and scar."

"Thank you. That's Mitchell Evans. He's been arrested for armed robbery before and recently came out of a short stint in prison for it. If we find him, I'll be sure that he is put away for much longer." The detective had me circle and sign the picture of the culprit, and then he stood and gathered all of the photos.

He handed me a card that had his details etched into the delicate paper. "Call me if you see him around. We will make sure the police officers in town are aware."

"Thank you, sir. I'll call if I see anything."

"I suggest getting lights for the doorway and a porch camera just in case. It's a safe neighborhood, but it doesn't stop these guys from taking a chance every now and then." He tilted his head before leaving.

The detective left, and after thanking Theresa, Grant, and his friends, they left too. Theresa had almost begged that I stay with her for the night just to be safe, but I said no. Grant disappeared into their car, and a moment later, he reemerged with a baseball bat. He handed it to me without saying a word, and I smiled in thanks. Once everyone was gone, I double-checked all the locks and windows in the apartment and went to bed. I would need to buy a new phone and apply for new bank cards the next morning because all of those things were in my purse. At this point, I couldn't cry anymore. This stuff kept happening. As soon as I was progressing with my life and things looked up, something bad would happen. I was mentally and emotionally exhausted, but I kept on pushing for Ricky's sake.

It had become apparent that I was struggling with traumainduced depression and anxiety. Mental illness wasn't something that was accepted or viewed as a real problem when I was younger. Even as an adult, it was hard to admit that I needed help, so I struggled through it and kept reminding myself that Ricky needed a mom and that my life mattered. It became harder to work through the bad experiences, and I would often struggle to get out of bed when Ricky went to visit Robert or Grandma. I felt lost and angry most days, and even though there were many good days, it always felt like there was a heaviness on my shoulders. It took longer to emotionally recover from things like the incident at home, but I couldn't bring myself to seek help from a professional. I just buried myself in work and being a good mom.

Two weeks later, while I was running errands with Ricky, I noticed the same man who attacked me driving a white van. The thing that angered me the most was that he was driving with his family in the van. I wondered if they knew what type of man he was, that he was a criminal. *What a terrible role model!* Those poor children. Hopefully, they wouldn't grow up like their father. I sent a prayer up to God for that exact thing.

I called the detective and the police. I gave them the license plate details and told them where I had seen him, and they advised that they would handle it. A few days later, the man was arrested on charges of armed robbery and attempted assault. He had tried to attack someone else, and this time, he was caught. Once he was locked up, I felt a lot more at ease. Theresa and Grant visited often, and he would still walk around the house when they arrived and before they left. Grant helped me install lights where I needed them, as well as the camera that I'd bought a few days earlier. The added security was a small consolation.

As soon as Ricky and I were completely settled in our house, we became more social. Ricky had a lot of friends, and I loved hosting sleepovers for them. We even hosted cookouts and game nights—a busy house felt more like home. Grandma and Papa came to visit at least once every two weeks. I hadn't heard from any of my siblings, and I often wished that I could share all of this with them. But every time I reached out, I received no response. I was glad that Mom seemed to have disappeared. In the beginning, after I left, she contacted Grandma often to find out where I was, but no one told her, thankfully. I didn't want her darkening this experience or our home. The last I heard was that she was a full-blown alcoholic and living with boyfriends or in shelters.

Ricky and I were invited to a cookout with Theresa. It was at one of her friends' houses, and Ricky was very excited that there would be children there for him to play with. He had grown into a social butterfly. After being such a quiet and shy kid, at some point, he just blossomed. He was such a special little boy, and I loved being his mom. It was amazing to see how big a difference a loving environment could make to a child.

We left for the cookout, and I parked in the street. There were a few cars lining the road up to the house, so I knew it would be a big event—Theresa loved the big cookouts. I left my bag in the car. It was a gift for myself that I had saved up months to buy; a Louis Vuitton, excessive but so beautiful. I felt proud every time I looked at it, and there was no way I was going to take the bag inside with me where it could be damaged. I squeezed it under my seat so that it wasn't visible and made sure the car was locked. The only thing I took inside with me was my cell phone and a bag of toys for the kids to play with.

It was a lovely afternoon, and Ricky played until he was exhausted. I met new people and spent the time chatting and making friends. It was one of the best cookouts that we had been to in months. Until we left...

I held Ricky in my arms, and he was starting to fall asleep against my shoulder. I walked to where I had parked my car and when I got there, it was gone. I wandered up and down the road to make sure I hadn't forgotten where I'd parked, and after a few minutes, it was clear that my car had been stolen. Out of all of the vehicles, mine was the one to be stolen.

"Theresa!" I yelled as my stomach sank.

Theresa came running, and I told her that my car was gone. This was two months after the incident with the man at my house. I called the police and followed the same process; except this time, I didn't know who had done it. I wanted to scream; I was so frustrated. After the initial commotion, it was discovered that one or two cars had been broken into as well. Whoever it was had stolen whatever valuables were available and drove off with my car. Theresa dropped us off at home, and I called insurance and everyone that I needed to. I was exhausted and angry, and I just wanted some peace. After sitting at my table for a few minutes, my stomach sank even more; the ring my grandma had given me as an heirloom had been in my bag. It was a beautiful, simple diamond ring, and I had eventually wanted to have it fitted when I got married. *If I ever got married...* But now it was gone, and I didn't think I would ever see it again.

Luckily, less than a week later, my car was found, along with the culprit. I was called to court, and when I arrived, the man didn't make eye contact. He just stared at the ground the entire time. I did, however, notice the woman sitting behind him. She looked to be his mother, and on her plump finger sat my diamond ring. I wanted to walk up to the man and slap him, and then I wanted to march over to her and rip the ring off of her finger. I told one of the officers about the ring, the bag was gone, but I wanted the ring back.

"Ma'am, where did you get the ring?" The officer asked the woman just before court ended.

"My... My son gave it to me," she said hesitantly.

"Please hand it over; it will need to be placed in evidence."

She reluctantly pulled the ring off of her finger and placed it in the waiting evidence bag. The man was sentenced for theft, and I got my ring back. He had sold my Louis Vuitton bag and gave his mother the ring as a gift. I was upset that the bag was gone but not as upset as I would have been if the ring had been lost forever. That same day, I bought a silver chain and wore the ring around my neck. It had huge sentimental value, and I wanted to hand it down to my daughter if I had one or to Ricky when he got married someday, as an engagement ring or something. It was the first time I ever had anything that I could hand down to my family. Once we left the house, Mom sold everything of value so that she could buy more alcohol, so there was no hope of having something to pass down from her.

The final bonus was that I also managed to get my car back, the man hadn't had the opportunity to sell it yet, or maybe he wanted to keep it for himself. It was amazing how filthy it was in the few days that it was in his possession, so I immediately took it to be cleaned. Work had been amazingly lenient when all of these things had happened. My boss had sent me home to make sure I had everything arranged and sorted after the robbery and the theft, which was a small piece of comfort. I was determined not to let anything get me down, I was upset and angry with the bad luck, but I tried to stay positive. I had an amazing support system, and even though I struggled with depression, it wasn't consuming me.

CHAPTER 10

MEN

My love life has been about as successful as the rest of my life; having to learn what love is after the way we grew up wasn't easy. There was a lot of trial and error, and I had to learn that I deserved to be treated well instead of just pleasing my partner. The first boyfriend I had after Robert was a disk jockey. John and I met at a bar one evening when Theresa and I went out. He was friendly and open and made me laugh, but the fact that he was well known in the area was a big adjustment for me. Whenever we went out for lunch or dinner, he would often be asked for photos or an autograph. He was a good player, and after a short while into our relationship, he became eager for me to meet his friends.

I never introduced him to Ricky. I didn't want my son to form an attachment with another man unless I was sure he would be a part of our lives for the long term, and after a few months, I still wasn't sure about John. He was a handsome man, he towered over me, and since he was an athlete, he was very strong. His eyes stood out to me. They were captivating and dark, but sometimes a little creepy, as if I could see into his soul, and I wasn't sure I'd like what I would find there. I wasn't sure, in the beginning, why I felt unsettled. He treated me extremely well, and he was a very loving man, but one evening after dinner, it became clear.

We'd had dinner at a fancy Italian restaurant, he had dressed particularly well that evening, and it was a good evening. After dinner, we headed back to his place so that I could get my car and head home. When we got to his place, as I gathered my coat and purse, he received a phone call. I couldn't hear much of it because he walked out of the kitchen while he was talking. When he came back, he said that he would be right there and hung up.

"Baby, I need to pick something up from a friend's house real quick. Would you please come with me? It's not far, and we won't be long," he says a minute later.

"It's late; I think I should rather go home."

"Come on; it won't take long. I don't want our date to end just yet." He insisted. I wanted to say no, but couldn't completely justify it, so we left in his car. Besides, I was working on trusting people more.

It was a short drive, and John told me more about his friend, which I thought was just small talk. "He's a good friend and a handsome man; you'll like him. He's a DJ and throws the best parties."

Chapter 10

Okay, strange. Why do I need to know that he's handsome? I felt a bit irritated, and I didn't feel like talking. I mistook the discomfort for irritation. Once again, I should have listened to my gut. We got to the house; it was more like a mansion, and the front door was massive. The size was evident, even from my seat in the car.

"Let's go; he's expecting me. We can have a drink and then head home," he said, placing his hand on my leg.

"I thought you were just dropping something off? I'm not really in a social mood tonight." The irritation was increasing; I just wanted to go home and curl up in bed. He batted his eyelashes at me, and I rolled my eyes. "Fine, just one drink."

We made our way to the door, and John knocked. I heard heavy footfalls on the other side, and in moments, an absolute giant opened the door. I looked up at him and caught myself thinking how John could say this man was handsome. He was huge, muscles protruding from his too-tight shirt and pants. I made a conscious effort not to pull my face. My gut lurched, and the discomfort finally registered. This man was staring at me as if I was a snack, and that familiar dirty feeling crept up. We went inside, and I stayed close to John. I didn't want to be alone with this giant.

"Take a seat. Can I get you something to drink?" The man asked. I didn't even register his name.

"Uh, no, thank you. I'm fine." *No way am I giving you the opportunity to drug me.* I sat down and crossed my arms. The leather chaise lounge was hard and a bit uncomfortable, so I shifted a bit as John sat down next to me.

In a second, he pulled me toward him and started kissing me. I pulled back in surprise and pushed on his chest. I knew he was affectionate, but I wasn't too interested in PDA, and it made me uncomfortable that this huge man was just standing there watching us. John's fingers fluttered toward the buttons on my blouse while trying to kiss me again. The giant sat down on a sofa in front of us and sipped his drink while watching us.

"What are you doing, John?" I asked, my voice hitching. "I thought you were just dropping something off."

He kissed my neck, and I shifted further from him. "Come on, baby. You said you wanted to come with me to visit my friend. We both just want to make you feel good."

"No, cut it out. I didn't agree to any of this. I didn't even want to come. I don't know what kind of sick game you're playing or what you're into, but I don't want any part of it." I stood up, and John followed. "Either you take me home, or I'll get a cab, but I'm not staying here for this."

I didn't give him a chance to answer and decided to call a cab. After calling, I walked out of the house to wait. Minutes later, a cab pulled up, and I gave him John's address. I collected my car, and I never saw John again.

After a short hiatus from dating, I met Jason. He was six years older than me and a military man. It was an emotional time for me because a few months prior, my father had made contact. He'd been speaking to me more and more, and eventually, he told me that he was dying and he wanted to make up for lost time. He admitted that he had kept his distance because of Mom and that she didn't want him to come close to us. I asked him to move in with Ricky and I, and it had been a relatively good experience, but it was a lot to get used to. When Jason came along, it was nice to have some support.

Jason was an amazing man; he was genuine, and I trusted him a lot quicker than most. We used to go dancing, and I laughed more than I had in my entire life. My father had retired from the military after 20 years of service, so when he met Jason, they spent hours and hours talking about the army and their service. They grew to love each other's company, and eventually, Ricky met him as well. He adored Jason and Jason was good with Ricky. They spent hours playing on a daily basis, and Ricky never wanted to say goodbye, so Jason would stay until after dinner and tuck him into bed.

Jason and I would often take the veterans who weren't able to drive to visit their families. It was a lovely experience, and they appreciated it. My father met Jason, and they hit it off immediately. They spoke about the war and where they were deployed, and I'd often walk in on them talking about what military life was like. My father often said that what kept him alive was whiskey, wine, and women, the three important W's. Jason took care of the old man while I was away on company travel. He'd make sure my father took his insulin shots, which he fussed about every time. Ricky would stay with Grandma, but he would spend a night or two with Jason and my father.

A few years later, my father passed away at the age of 83. I cried and mourned for a long time. I cried for all the years that we missed because of my narcissistic mom. I cried because it was the best short five years with my father. I was glad that Ricky had the opportunity to meet his grandfather. Jason was my rock through that time, but the military made a relationship extremely hard. They started deploying him to further places for longer periods of time, and eventually, we decided to go our separate ways. We remained good friends, and he kept in contact with Ricky as well. Our relationship had been one of the best, and sometimes I wished that it hadn't ended, but I knew it was better for both of us to move on. We were better as friends at the end of the day.

Coming back from the best relationship, I then had my worst experience. Worse than what happened with Sampson and the bad luck that we went through. I landed a job with an insurance firm run by a husband-and-wife team. There were a few other staff members, and it was a smaller firm, but they were successful, and the pay and perks were really good. The first month was great, I got along well with everyone in the company, and the work was interesting. At the end of my first month, I'd gotten into an accident, a drunk driver collided with my car, and it was a write-off. Luckily, I didn't have any bad injuries, and I was back at work after a week. I was waiting for my insurance to pay out so that I could buy a new car, so Theresa dropped me off in the morning on the first day back.

Everyone was welcoming and showed genuine concern, and I had a great first day back. I made a high amount of insurance sales which placed me on the CEO, Damon's radar.

"Well done, you seem to be catching on quick. I didn't expect that from a rookie." He joked; he walked with me to the door.

"Thank you, Damon." I beamed at him; acknowledgment was always nice. "Anyway, let me call my friend quickly. She needs to pick me up. No car..." I turned to speak to Theresa, but he placed his hand on my arm.

"Don't worry about it; I'm headed out now too. I can give you a ride." He opened the door for me.

I walked through and fiddled with my phone. Damon had been a mentor so far, and I was learning so much from him, but I didn't want him to think I was taking advantage. "If you're sure, I don't want to be a nuisance."

He shook his head, and we made our way to his fancy black BMW. He seemed like a good man. He was always polite and professional. I would never have thought that a monster lurked beneath. I climbed in, and the seats hugged me. It was luxurious. "Nice car, boss," I said with a smile.

He laughed. "Thanks, she drives like a dream. Where do you live?"

I gave him my address, and he nodded as we pulled away. "I need to stop by my house on the way to pick up some gear for a friend. Is that okay with you?"

I didn't want to say no and seem pushy, so I nodded. A short drive later, we pulled up to a beautiful brick face home.

It's big, and it looks like the perfect family home. It looked like it was one of the older homes that had been renovated with multiple floors and quaint white window frames. It screamed vintage elegance, and it was close to what I'd imagined as my dream home.

"You can come in." He said as he climbed out of the car.

"I'm okay in the car. I don't want to intrude."

"I won't be long. Come in. I think my wife is here, and she'd love to see you too. You can tell her about those sales figures."

I nodded and laughed. We made our way to the house, and Damon unlocked the door to reveal an elegant entrance with a marble table and a bold staircase leading to the second level. Everything was immaculately clean.

"Take a seat. Do you want a drink? I have the bar all stocked up." He motioned to a bar in the corner by the living room.

I shook my head. "No thanks, I don't drink."

His eyebrows shot up. "Suit yourself." He moved into the kitchen and placed his jacket and keys on the counter. I followed him.

"Where's your wife? I thought she would be here," I asked, looking around. It didn't look like anyone was home.

"I guess she isn't. She took the kids on vacation for the week." He turned and looked at me intensely while he undid his tie. The familiar feeling settled in my stomach.

"Why did you say she would be here?" I asked hesitantly.

He took a step closer and unbuttoned the first few buttons of his shirt. "I wanted to get you alone. I wanted you to myself."

I took a step back. "No, you don't. You're my boss, and I think I'm ready to go home now." I tried to edge toward the door.

"I know you want me, Naomi. I see the way you look at me. I want you too." The words were meant to sound seductive, but they came out as a sneer.

"I don't know what you are talking about, Damon. This is a mistake. Take me home, now!" Panic was rising, and my voice wobbled.

He kept approaching like a predator circling his prey, and I was his prey. My only exit was behind him, and I tried to figure out how to get past him. The kitchen counter hit my hip. Before I could say anything else, he reached toward me and grabbed my neck. I grabbed at his fingers as he started to choke me. His face was close to mine. I could feel his warm breath on my lips as he ran the fingers of his free hand over my breast. He groaned as his hand traveled lower to the edge of my dress. His fingers edged under my dress, and I squirmed again. I heard the zipper from his pants. Suddenly, Damon started to drag me across the floor to the huge sofa in their TV room. I kicked and wriggled, but he was much stronger than me.

"I know you want me. You're lying to yourself." It was becoming harder to breathe. As he dragged me past the bar, I managed to grab a bottle. It was heavy, and I hoped it would work.

He dropped me on the floor and dropped his pants. I took that moment to swing the bottle back and hit him on his head. The glass shattered, and Damon stumbled, grabbing his head with both hands.

"You heifer! Oh, you like it rough. I'll show you how rough I can be." He snarled and reached for me. As he grasped the front of my dress, I pulled away and ran to the front door. It was locked. Damon had locked the door when we came inside. I turned and ran to the patio door. He was right behind me. Damon had turned into a mad man. He was not the same man I had grown to know. Who was he? A monster.

I burst through the door and ran for my life, my dress was torn and hanging off my shoulder, and my throat burned, but I kept running. As if sent by God, a police car drove past and stopped when I waved him down. I climbed into the car and breathed for a minute as the officer rubbed my back. Shakily, I told him what had happened. He handed me a jacket so that I could cover myself.

"My purse is in his car. I can't go back." I sobbed.

The officer called his partner, and when he arrived, they made their way to Damon's house, where he was apprehended and taken to the station. The officer returned to the car with my purse. I sobbed all the way home. I had no doubt that he would have killed me. Damon would have raped and killed me. My neck was bruised, my clothes were torn, and I was terrified.

The officer dropped me off at home and gave me his direct number if I needed urgent help. I filed an incident report with him and thanked him. I spent over an hour in the shower trying to scrub the experience off of me. After questioning, I was contacted three months later and told to go to court. Damon was found guilty of abduction, assault, and attempted rape, and he was sentenced to eight years in prison.

After a long and painful period of healing from the incident with Damon, I met my first husband, Andrew. My first marriage was a fairytale in the beginning. Andrew was everything I wanted in a partner. He was a loving husband and an amazing father. He paid a lot of attention to Ricky, and I thought this was finally the family I wanted. Early into our marriage, we had a beautiful daughter, Emma. Ricky loved being a big brother, and he always wanted to help when it came to his baby sister. Ricky and I had moved into a bigger apartment before I met Andrew, and after we got married, he moved in with us. We were married for nine years, but everything started to crumble after the first two years. We started arguing more, and Andrew spent more time away from home.

Closer to the end of our marriage, I started having vivid dreams of Andrew cheating and that he'd gotten another woman pregnant, and for a long time, I tried to shake the feeling. They started to feel more like visions instead of dreams, and I was starting to drive myself crazy, so I decided to speak to Andrew about it. He told me I was overreacting and completely denied everything. So, I asked him where he was spending all of his time. He would go to work or the store and come back a day later. During that time, his phone would be off, and when he got back home, he would say that his phone had died and he had drinks with a male friend from work, and he didn't want to drive home drunk.

I was suspicious from the first time, but he was so good at manipulation that I would convince myself that I was being ridiculous and that he loved us, so he would never do something like that. After I spoke to him about the pregnancy visions, he started acting strange. He grew even more distant, and eventually, two weeks before Christmas, our marriage ended in the worst way.

I arrived home from work one afternoon before picking the children up from school, and the apartment was almost completely bare. Andrew took the bed, a sofa, and most of the other furniture. He didn't answer his phone or respond to messages, and I eventually found out that he had, in fact, gotten another woman pregnant, and he had moved out to live with her.

I broke down and cried in my half-empty apartment. Nine years of my life were wasted. The best thing I got from our marriage was Emma, and I had no idea how I would explain to her and Ricky that Andrew wasn't coming back. I was once again alone and tired of the heartbreak.

"What did I do to deserve this life?" I yelled into the empty space. I asked Theresa to pick the children up, and she did without asking questions.

I sat on the floor and cried until I couldn't anymore. I had no idea how I would build up from this again. I sank into a deep depression. I sent money to Theresa after she offered to take care of the children for a few days. On one of the worst days, words filled my mind, the voice was bitter, and I knew it was the devil whispering into my left ear, filling my head with negative thoughts. *Who's going to love you with two children? Just end it all; no one loves you. There's a bottle of pills in the bathroom, just take them all and fall asleep; it won't even hurt.* I walked over to the bathroom and held the bottle in my hand. I wanted to; I wanted it to end. I looked at myself in the mirror; I was a mess. My hair was knotted, and I had dark circles under my eyes. I opened the bottle and spilled the contents into my hand. Suddenly a sense of calm filled me; a peaceful voice entered my thoughts. I love you, child. I looked at my reflection again in confusion. *Just take the pills; cut your wrists! You don't want this anymore.* The darkness tried to cut through the peace, and I cried out, "Darkness will not live here! I won't let it!"

I will never leave you, child; you need to fight. Your children depend on you; no one can love them the way you do. Don't give up; you are destined for greatness! It was God; I knew it. His words were gentle and kind, and they pushed the darkness away. I could finally see more clearly than I had in days. I dropped the pills down the drain and thanked God. I pulled myself together and picked Emma and Ricky up immediately. We would get through this together.

Months later, Andrew tried to crawl back in, but with renewed strength, I sent him away. I refused to allow him back into my life. He had visitation with the children, but that was the extent of the contact. I was present at every single visit, and eventually, he stopped asking for them. Emma was heartbroken, but I gently explained that it was his loss and he wasn't worth her tears. I made a concerted effort to make sure my children knew that they were loved beyond measure.

CHAPTER 11

STEPPING UP

After my marriage to Andrew, I worked hard to get my real estate license and eventually opened my own agency. It took a long time, but it turned into a major success. The three of us moved into a proper house, we had so much more space, and Emma and Ricky had their own rooms. During the divorce and moving, I found out that I was pregnant. I was a few months along and hadn't suspected a thing. Being a mother was the biggest blessing of my life, and my two children had saved my life more than once. After many emotional rollercoasters and complete denial from Andrew, I had my third child, a baby girl. Emma was ecstatic, and initially, Ricky was upset that he didn't have a brother, but he warmed up to baby Lily. Even though the marriage had ended badly, I walked away with two incredible girls.

I made a point of giving back to the community by volunteering at the senior home in the area. I tried to make the seniors' day a little brighter by helping them do arts & crafts as well as lessons with computers and technology. I loved my time with them, and seeing their excitement and creating relationships with each of them was the most rewarding part. I was there whenever I had some extra time.

The children and I adopted a dog who became a huge part of our family. Bucky was the definition of man's best friend, and I took him everywhere with me. I started taking him to the seniors, and they adored him. He received treats on every visit, which he loved, and in return, he got them laughing and smiling. I finally felt like my family was complete. I tried not to think about the negative times, and I lived life wholly through God. My faith and my children had saved me on numerous occasions. I still struggled with mental illness, but I learned to cope with it instead of feeling overwhelmed by it.

The kids weren't without their challenges. Ricky was diagnosed with severe ADHD, but with a lot of patience and effort, he managed to overcome the worst of it. He moved out after-school and managed to land a position as a manager for a large clothing company. He became very successful and climbed the ladder quite fast. Emma followed her dreams and became a writer and a performer. I knew she would. She was a little actress from a young age. Lily followed in her footsteps and started her own clothing line while she was still in school. I felt incredibly proud of all three of them.

I started counseling at the schools and support centers. I used my experience to help others that had been through the same things. I worked hard to help others, and eventually, once my real estate company was in capable hands, I delved into being a lawyer since I'd received my qualifications years ago, and I knew I would be able to help more people. My most memorable experience of being a lawyer was with a young man named Jack.

He was 27 years old, and at that time, there was a controversial case against a camp counselor from years before. I was requested to be on the case when I found out that it involved sexual abuse against minors. It was highly sensitive, but a few people came forward when the story broke. When Jack was younger, he'd attended a summer camp, and he retold the emotional story of his innocence that had been stolen. He was in primary school, and his sister was meant to go with him. However, she was no longer allowed to go due to family issues. The first few days were great, they had a lot of fun, and every day was filled with exciting activities and the usual camp games. One afternoon, Jack stayed behind to help one of the camp counselors, a young man, with tidying up. He was a friendly guy, one of the favorites around the camp, and Jack had never felt uncomfortable around him. But for some reason, that afternoon was different.

Jack couldn't place his finger on why he felt the way he did, so he ignored it and chalked it up to being tired from all the fun they'd had that day. The camp counselor was his usual friendly self, making small talk and asking questions about Jack and what he enjoyed doing at home. They ended up in the small supply closet while packing the last things away, and this was when the man changed. He closed the door and made Jack do things that no child ever should. It didn't go as far as intercourse, but it was enough to leave Jack traumatized. The counselor kept Jack in the closet for what felt like hours. Eventually, he dressed himself and left Jack in the closet with the insistence that they did nothing wrong and that no one would believe him if he spoke about it. It wasn't a direct threat, but the undertone was there. Jack sat in the closet until well after dark. He cried and held himself in a tight ball until he got his emotions under control. He knew what had happened was wrong, but he couldn't make sense of it, much like my experience with Blair.

After the encounter, Jack tried to keep his distance. The activities and games were no longer fun, and everything had a gloominess to it. He used the excuse of feeling sick on most days, especially when they had an activity planned with the counselor. The children eventually had a chance to speak to their parents on a call, and Jack wanted to ask his parents if he could go home. They had just short of a week left, and he hoped that his parents would understand even though they had spent money to send him to camp. He built up the courage, but when his mom answered, he thought of what his dad would do.

Jack and his sister grew up in a very hard household, their father was an impatient man, and he often took his frustration out on them. He was much harder on Jack's sister and often beat them in the name of discipline, but sometimes he would leave bruises, and as they grew older, Jack knew that wasn't normal. His mom knew about the beatings, but she never intervened, most likely out of fear that his anger would be turned on her. Thinking of what his reaction would be, Jack decided to keep quiet. The rest of the camp was tainted with darkness, and Jack didn't enjoy anything. He kept to himself and skipped out on as many of the activities as he could. All the friends he had made eventually stopped trying to get him to join them, and he was left alone. He saw the camp counselor, but made sure to keep his distance when he was around, and he never engaged in conversation.

That year, a few people came forward with the same allegations. Jack saw a notice one evening on his TV while watching the news where it was requested that anyone else who had similar stories come forward and testify so that he could be locked up for a long, long time. That's when Jack called, and the court arranged a meeting with me. I was determined to help, to get this man in prison and give Jack some semblance of justice. His innocence would never recover, but knowing the man was behind bars would make coping a bit easier. We built up our case, and a week later, we were called in to testify. Jack sat by my side, and he handled the pressure well. He faced the man, now much older that had done horrible things years ago to him and to others. The man didn't look up once unless he was addressed by the judge. Anger filled Jack's face, and I understood the feeling when the person who had made such a terrible impact on your life couldn't even look you in the eye. From experience, it made you want to walk up to him and force him to look at you, to see the pain and suffering he had inflicted. Once Jack testified, court was put on hold for the final verdict. We stood outside the doors and waited to be called back in. Jack paced up and down the corridor, and I reiterated that he had done an amazing job, that the man would be found guilty, and Jack could move on with his life knowing that he'd had a hand in putting him in jail.

I felt a tap on my shoulder and spun. "Are you... Is your name Naomi?" The woman in front of me asked; she looked familiar.

She was around my age and shared a resemblance to Jack. "Yes?" I answered.

She smiled, and I struggled to place her. "It's lovely to see you. It's Sarah, from middle school. I'm Jack's sister."

The familiarity finally made sense. Her skin was the same tanned caramel color. Her skin had cleared from the acne, and she looked beautiful. She was a bit plumper than I remembered, but she carried an air of confidence. Her smile was warm and kind, completely opposite to the scowl she used to wear at school.

"Oh, Sarah! I had no idea that you and Jack were related. He spoke about you but never mentioned a name. How have you been?" I asked.

"Good, thanks. I just wanted to thank you for helping Jack. We were all shocked when the story came out and when Jack told us that he was one of the victims." She smiled, and her eyes glazed over a bit. She shuffled uncomfortably. "I also wanted to say sorry. You know, for all those years at school. I was a terrible person, and it took a while, but I realized that you didn't deserve it. I hope you can forgive me."

It felt like a weight had been lifted off of my shoulders. "Of course! I forgave you a long time ago, but I appreciate the apology."

I didn't realize until then how much I wanted to hear her apologize. She played such a big part in my unhappiness at school and so many others. But as I grew up, I pushed it aside, and after lots of prayers, I'd forgiven her. A certain calm settled over me once I did, and, in my heart, I knew that Sarah had been facing so much more than what everyone assumed was just bad behavior. After that day in the office and then speaking to Jack, my suspicions were confirmed. Her father was about as bad as my mom. I felt like I understood Sarah more.

One of the officers came into the foyer and let us know that the verdict had been made. Everyone was led back into the courtroom, and we were told to take our seats. I smiled at Jack encouragingly. The judge entered, and one of the court officers took the note from the judge to be read aloud to everyone who had gathered for the testimonies. The camp counselor was found guilty. He was sentenced to 35 years in prison with no chance of parole for the crimes he committed against the kids at the summer camp. There was a unified sigh of relief in the room, and the other victims that were there were crying silently, tears of joy and relief. The press cameras went off, and photos of the man who ruined so many young lives would be published in the morning paper. All of his victims were offered six months of counseling which was funded by a major corporation. A little while later, we found out that the counselor hadn't even lasted six months in jail; one of the other inmates found out that he had committed sex crimes against children and killed him on prison grounds.

Once we all left the court, Sarah stopped me again and invited me for coffee to thank me for helping Jack. I agreed, and we spent the afternoon at a local coffee shop. Jack finished his coffee, thanked me, and left. I was sure it would take some time for him to process the events of the day, and quiet was what he needed. Sarah and I spoke for hours, and I found myself enjoying her company, which was a surprise after all the issues we had in middle school. She had grown into an outstanding woman who tried to right the wrongs she'd made. She was an active member of the community and worked in social services.

From the many conversations that Jack and I had, I knew that life at home back then wasn't good. I figured that was what triggered the bullying, and I felt sorry for her, but now I was glad that she had turned her life around. She told me about her father and that he had passed away a year prior. Once she and Jack had left the house, they stopped talking to him and their mother. Their mother didn't help them at all, and only after their father had died did she try and reach out to them to "make amends," but in earnest, she didn't have a job or any money, and he hadn't left anything behind for her. Sarah sent her some money so that she could stay afloat, but she didn't maintain a relationship. We became close friends and often enjoyed lunch or coffee together. We somehow bonded over our sad and abusive upbringing.

I remarried eight years after the court case. Phil was a pastor at the local church, and after a challenging start with my trust issues and doubt, I realized his love was genuine. He was always there to reassure me that I deserved love and happiness, especially when I had hard days. We maintained a relationship for two years before he asked me to marry him. The engagement was incredible, Phil took me on a helicopter ride over the mountains, and after a breathtaking trip, we landed on a clearing where a picnic had been laid out for us. We went on little adventures often, not as extravagant as that, but I didn't expect a thing. While I was picking flowers and exploring the area, Phil poured two glasses of champagne, and as I turned toward him, he was kneeling on one knee with a gorgeous ring nestled in a velvet case. I cried and laughed and held him tight. I didn't think I could be happier.

Getting married so late in life was never in my plans. I was nearing my mid-forties at that point, and I had come to terms with the fact that I probably wouldn't get married again. But once again, God showed me that He had His own plans, and even though mine didn't work out the way I wanted them to, He knew when the right time would come about.

Phil and I stayed in our separate homes because he wanted to live together once we were married. Emma was finishing school at the end of the year that we got engaged, and Lily was still in high school. Emma decided that she wanted to go to college to study acting, and she would be off at the beginning of the next year. Living separately gave Lily a chance to get used to having Phil around. He was an amazing father to all three of my children. Ricky was living on his own, making a success of his life. He visited often and lived a distance away in a different city. He loved Phil, and since Phil never had children of his own, Ricky was the son he had always wanted. Emma took to him well, and he helped her enroll in a good college in New York. It was far away, and I was incredibly emotional at the thought of having her in a different city. We would have to fly to visit, but her heart was set on NYU's drama course, and after a lot of convincing, I agreed to it. Lily was at the typical teenager stage, she was never disrespectful or rude, but she kept to herself. Phil adjusted to it and continued to make an effort. She started making clothes in middle school, and by the time she was in high school, she was really good at it. Phil bought her a sewing machine, and he made an effort to learn about design. Lily was set to release her own clothing line at the local mall by the end of high school. She already had scholarship offers to a few fashion schools, and we made sure to encourage her to follow her dreams.

Once we were engaged, I asked Phil to move in with us after the wedding. The house was close to his church, and it was big enough for all of us. Lily felt most comfortable there, so he agreed without hesitation. We decided to host an engagement party a week after Phil popped the question, and I roped Emma into the planning and decor. I had an important surprise planned for the party. It was a private surprise, but Ricky, Emma, and Phil helped make it special.

CHAPTER 12

LOVE AND MARRIAGE

The engagement party rolled around, and Ricky came for a few nights to celebrate with us. He adored his sisters, and every time he visited, he brought a few gifts for them. For Emma, he often got his hands-on old movie scripts or memorabilia, and for Lily, he made sure to buy materials and design magazines. I loved that they had such great relationships. I'd invited my siblings to the engagement, but I didn't receive a response except from Jackie, who promised to be at the wedding, but she and her boyfriend were traveling, so they couldn't make it to the engagement party. I was happy that after the intervention, Jackie stayed sober. She relapsed once or twice but always managed to find her feet. Theresa came with Grant, who was now her husband; their wedding had been fabulous. She was heavily pregnant with their second child. Papa had sent a message to say that, unfortunately, Grandma was unwell, and he was taking care of her. They sent a massive bouquet of flowers in their stead. Sarah went to check on Grandma before she got to the party. When she arrived, she told me that Grandma was asleep and Papa was watching over her. Everything was okay.

The party went off without a hitch, Phil's close friends from the church joined us, and it was a jolly affair. Later that evening, I was chatting to Ricky when a clinking filled the room. Everyone fell silent as Phil stood on the podium set up in the middle of the room. He looked dashing in a navy suit, his greying hair slicked back and a smile on his face. He was a good-looking man, Phil went running every day and kept us on a healthy diet, and it showed. He had a lean body, the muscles in his legs rippled when he walked, and his arms were strong and tanned. We spent a lot of our free time outdoors— hiking, fishing, or boating. Even my fair skin had gained some color from the sun.

"Excuse me!" He cleared his throat, and all eyes were on him. "I know there were no speeches planned, but I do love surprises. I won't keep you from the festivities for long." Light laughter filled the room, and I smiled at Phil. He winked at me and continued. "I wanted to thank you all for taking the time to join us. If you told me three years ago that I would be here with my soon-tobe wife, I would have laughed. I spent many days speaking to God, asking Him if I would ever meet the right woman and His answer was always clear. *'Not yet, my son.'* I accepted that it may not be in God's plan and that it was my destiny to preach His word, and that's where my love would be. I was happy with that, but now I know that not yet didn't mean never. It meant that the time would come when

God knew that I was ready. Tonight, my heart is full. And it's all because of my beautiful fiancée, Naomi." Phil looked at me. "Naomi, we may have met a little later in life than we expected, but it was God's plan. You are an incredible woman, and I feel grateful every single day that I get to love you. You are beautiful and kind, selfless and brave. I cannot imagine my life without you in it. You taught me patience and empathy, and through you, I have inherited three amazing children." His gaze moved to where Ricky, Emma, and Lily were sitting. "I may not have had a hand in raising you, your mother did that brilliantly before we found each other, but I hope you will allow me to say that I feel blessed to have each of you in my life. Your mother and I may not be married yet, but I see you three as my children, maybe not through blood but through love."

Emma wiped a tear from her cheek, and even Lily looked as if she wanted to cry. Ricky beamed at Phil, and my heart wanted to explode. Phil cleared his throat again. "With that, let's enjoy the rest of the celebration. Naomi, I love you!"

Clapping filled the room as Phil made his way toward me. I wrapped him in a big hug, and when I let go, my children were there. Ricky hugged him as well, and so did Emma. Lily smiled, she wasn't one for affection, but she squeezed Phil's hand.

"That was sweet." She said softly.

Phil nodded and squeezed back.

"On that note, Lily, I have something for you," I said as Ricky handed me a little box.

She looked at me with a frown. "What's that?"

"Open it."

Lily opened the box, and her hand flew to her mouth. "Mom, really?!"

Tears filled my eyes as she held onto the small piece of lace fabric, a piece from Grandma's old wedding dress. I'd used it to cover a delicate note. *Lily, my sweet, talented girl. Will you please make my wedding dress?*

"Of course, I will! But are you sure? I'm still practicing," she said, unsure of herself.

"I'm certain. You have a gift, and I know it will be beautiful. I wouldn't want anyone else to do it."

Lily pulled me into a big hug, which was unlike her, but I savored it. She nodded into my shoulder. It was decided then. Lily would do the wedding dress, Emma would arrange the music, and Ricky would be the MC.

"Let's enjoy the rest of the evening," I said.

And so, we did. We danced and laughed, sang and ate until it was almost midnight. I was excited to see what our future held.

We decided to have the wedding six months after the engagement and all of my free time went into planning, booking the venue, dress fittings, and sending invitations out. We hired a wedding planner to help with the decor and food. Sarah was a huge help during the six months. She was there every step of the way. Days after the engagement party, I took her out to lunch and arranged with the server to give her a champagne flute that I had engraved. *Will you be my maid of honor?* Sarah didn't notice until we were two glasses in. She stared at the words for a few minutes and suddenly jumped up, spilling the liquid all over the table.

"Yes! Of course!" She gushed.

From that day, she had taken on all the stressful details. She organized the kitchen tea and many other things that I didn't have the time to get to. She was an absolute blessing.

Three weeks before the wedding, I received devastating news. Papa came over unexpectedly, and I knew before he said anything that Grandma had passed away. My heart shattered. I'd visited her often, and in the past weeks, it seemed like she was getting better. She had lung cancer, and by the time the doctor picked it up, it had already progressed too far. Grandma agreed to chemo, and she handled it really well, but she knew she was dying. Her last wish was to be at the wedding, that's why we set the date at six months. I was with her two days before she passed, and she was her old perky self. I prayed that she would make it, and it seemed like my prayers were being answered, but Papa said that early that morning, her lungs gave in. She died in her sleep peacefully.

I cried and cried until I had no more tears. I knew she was with God and wasn't suffering anymore, and that was my consolation. Her funeral took precedent, and I made sure to give her the best send-off that I could. No one wore black. It was requested that everyone come in her favorite colors to celebrate her life. And through the tears, we did. She was the mother I should have had. A hard, old lady but filled with love.

The wedding day arrived, and it was the most incredible day of my life. Phil pulled out all the stops, and I was able to have the wedding of my dreams. Lily had spent every free hour stuck in her room making my dress. The only time I saw it was when she took my measurements to adjust the size closer to the wedding day. I finally got to see the finished product on the day when she helped me get into it. It was exquisite, completely unique, and I was once again amazed at her skill. The dress was made with white chiffon and had the most beautiful pearls sewn into the fragile material. The train was a few feet long and elegant, and the bodice fit like a corset. The whole dress made me feel like a princess. The rhinestone and bead encrusted headpiece completed the look. Once it was on and the corset strapped, I noticed a small piece of material over my heart that looked slightly different.

"What's this?" I asked, touching the piece that was almost unnoticeable.

Lily smiled. "Since Grandma can't be here in person, I thought I'd keep her here in spirit. It's the piece of her gown that you gave to me when you asked me to make the dress. Now she will be with you."

That did it; I sobbed at the thought. Lily made a dress that was far better than I expected, far more sentimental than it already was. I was relieved that I hadn't had my makeup done yet because it would have washed away with my tears. Once I pulled myself together, the makeup artist placed a cover over my shoulder to protect the material and got to work on my makeup. I chose a natural makeup look that made my fair skin shimmer.

It felt like a moment in a movie as I entered the ceremony venue, the guests lining the aisle fell silent, and they watched in admiration as I made my way to the altar. Soft sighs mixed with the swishing from the train following behind me. I looked at Phil, and his eyes were filled with tears; I felt the pure love emanating from him, and tears threatened to spill. I took a deep breath, thinking about the makeup that had been done just before and not wanting to ruin it. I felt beautiful and loved; it made all the hardships from my past worth the wait for true love. The only thing I wished for was that I had met Phil earlier. I placed a hand over the material on my heart, and I truly felt complete.

The wedding itself was memorable, we chose a venue that overlooked a huge lake, and since it was summer, the trees and bushes around the venue were in full bloom, adding to the beauty. It was tranquil and calm. The venue had a stunning old church close to the reception area, which made it easier for the guests to get there after the ceremony. The stone church was beautiful on its own, but my wedding planner had lined the aisle with lilies and vines, and we had Theresa's daughter throw flower petals as I walked in.

The reception was decorated in much the same way. I wanted to make everything look like it had a bit of nature drawn in from the outside. I'd never been happier than on our wedding day. Phil was handsome in a navy tux. Ricky stood next to him as his groomsman, and on the opposite side of the altar stood Sarah. She'd become an amazing support for my children and me, even though they were all older now. She looked gorgeous; her dark hair pulled up into a loose bun with strands gently caressing her face. She wore a floor-length navy dress that perfectly hugged all of her curves. She smiled brightly as I made my way down the aisle to Phil. Next to her were Emma and Lily. They were beautiful in matching navy dresses, similar to Sarah's.

My gaze swept to my soon-to-be husband, tears trickled down his cheeks, and his gaze was fixed on me. I felt beautiful; I knew I looked beautiful, but his reaction solidified it. He looked at me as if I were the only woman in the world, and for a moment, everyone else disappeared, and it was just Phil and I in the church. My heart fluttered.

Papa walked me down the aisle. He was crying quietly as I held on to his arm. I wished Grandma was there, I wished that she could give me a hug and tell me that she was proud of me, but I knew she was watching from above. Papa handed me to Phil, and we said our vows. Everything was perfect, and I would remember this day forever.

After the ceremony, the guests made their way to the reception area. Phil and I and the children had our photos taken and then joined everyone else. The reception was everything I could dream of. Emma played the piano and sang while Ricky kept everyone happy and engaged. We sat down for dinner, and then the time for speeches rolled around. Phil stood from his seat next to me, and the room fell silent.

Chapter 12

"Welcome, and thank you for coming. It feels like a lifetime ago since I saw you all at our engagement party. A lot has changed since then, so I would like to start off with a moment of silence for a gentle soul who is no longer with us but who I know is celebrating with God. To Grandma, you are dearly missed." Everyone closed their eyes, and silence fell for a few minutes. "I'm going to keep this short and sweet. Naomi, you are the woman of my dreams. I am the luckiest man alive to be seated next to you as your husband. You look beautiful every day, and today, you are breathtaking. I adore you, and I promise to be a safe haven and support for you from now on. God really outdid himself when he allowed me to be your husband." Phil wiped at his eyes and cleared his throat. "To my three God-gifted children, I am blessed to have met you and to be in your lives. You three did an incredible job today. You are my family, and I couldn't be happier. Please raise a glass to my wife and family."

Everyone clinked their glasses in a toast. I dabbed at the tears that had spilled from Phil's speech and kissed him lovingly as he sat down again. A few more people made speeches, and then it was time for our first dance. It was magical, and it once again felt like we were the only two people in the room.

The rest of the evening went by in a blur of dancing and celebration. Before long, it was time to retire, my feet were aching, and my voice was hoarse. I'd cried happy tears until I had no more to cry. Phil carried me to our room for the night and laid me down gently on the soft bed. He helped me out of my dress, and we spent the rest of the night getting lost in each other. It was the perfect ending to the perfect day.

We said goodbye to our guests the next morning and set off on a two-week honeymoon. The first week was an adventure in a caravan. We travelled through forests and camped in the wilderness, and we caught fish and cooked it on the fire. The days were lazy and invigorating. We slowly made our way to the coast, where we spent the last week on a cruise. Phil and I were completely enamored with each other, and the trip was an absolute bliss. We were well rested by the time we got back home, and, in the weeks following our return, Phil moved in with Lily and me, and we spent time unpacking and getting used to living together. We took Emma to college, helped her settle in, and after an emotional goodbye, we made the trip back home and settled into our new life.

This was what I'd always wanted, a family that loved each other, and I knew that God gave me the challenges in my past to mold me into the person I had become. I felt like my life was just beginning, and I was ready to use the lessons that I had learned to help others. I wanted to share my experiences so that other people didn't feel like they were alone. I opened up to Phil completely. I told him about Mom and my childhood, about every experience I had and how I got through them. He was supportive and loving, and I never felt judged. I decided to get help for my depression and anxiety, which was very much present in my life even though everything was going well. Although it was difficult in the beginning, the sessions helped me learn how to work through every experience. I

Chapter 12

learned how to get through depressive episodes and panic attacks, it was an eye-opening journey, and I kept my faith through it all.

CHAPTER 13

SUPPORT

Phil was supportive in all of my endeavors and dreams. After everything that had happened with Blair, Sampson, Brock, and Damon, I wanted to build a place where other women and children could come for shelter. I had a hard time at home with Mom and all the abuse that she put me through, and I knew that many children experienced the same thing. I knew women experienced abuse at the hands of their partners on a daily basis, as well as sexual abuse toward children occurred numerous times every day. I wanted to create somewhere where these people could come to if they had no other way to escape. I would have run away to a place like that if there was one back in the day, and I knew it would go a long way to help women and mothers get back on their feet again. I wanted to work closely with the court and use my influence as a lawyer so that the perpetrators could be brought to justice when the victims felt ready to talk.

I spoke to Sarah. She'd gone through abuse at the hands of her father and knew what it was like to have to live with it as a child, so she was the perfect partner in this venture. We started making plans. I confronted a few of my friends in the court and organized meetings to discuss how we could work together to help. We decided to build a home where at least four families could live with a daycare on site for the mothers who needed to work. We would also have a job support center and a canteen where they could eat for free. The home would be the halfway point where these people could find their way back to a good life without worrying about costs. Phil was fully supportive and helped us build the home with his savings, as well as mine and Sarah's.

It took a lot of our time and money to have the drawings done, pay contractors and builders, and then make sure it was completed to the level of quality I was determined to have. Sarah and I approached the local organization's support offices and asked for funding in order to keep the home going. We would put all of our available funds into it, but it was important to have the city behind us so that we could make it a safe haven for many years to come. The idea was that we would host events, and the public could make donations to help the home.

After a few weeks of up and down, of stating our plans and how we planned to make sure it was a success, the city gave us the funding. They gave us a support officer who would be there to oversee the progress once the women and children started living there. I would assist by being a counselor on the property, and they would also pay me a wage to do this. It was a huge relief. Sarah and I proceeded at full steam to get the home built and completed. After a handful of meetings with the court, I managed to get the support we needed to defend the victims once they were prepared to put their abusers behind bars. Another important factor was security, since many abusers went after their victims, especially in domestic violence cases. We made sure that we would have cameras on the perimeter of the home and a direct emergency contact with the security company.

It took just over a year for everything to be prepared. The rooms were fully furnished with comfortable and homey decor and furnishings. The canteen was fully stocked, and we had a stream of volunteers that wanted to help with the cooking and general work around the home. The job center was filled with computers and job resources, as well as a contact person who would help find good jobs for the mothers. Sarah worked in the daycare; she loved taking care of the children. She made sure the daycare always had fun toys and activities that would keep the children busy and excited. It was a place where they could finally be children again and just enjoy the things that were taken from them due to abuse or any other bad situation that they'd been in. There was a ribbon cutting ceremony with the mayor of the town on opening day, and we hosted a tour of the facility along with delicious food afterward. A beautiful statue had been donated anonymously of a woman holding a baby. We placed it in the front yard, and it was the first thing people would see when they arrived. I named the facility "Pearl's Place," and I wanted it to be a beacon of faith and safety in the community.

We created an application system after the first opening because of the influx of people that needed help. The rooms were filled, and we were very busy with counseling and taking care of those in our care. The local news picked up on our home and decided to feature us in the next newspaper as well as broadcast on TV. It was an incredible feeling, and donation lines were opened. We received a huge amount of support over the first few months. We were able to support the volunteers with food. There were so many that we had to implement a rotation system, but we were so grateful that people wanted to be a part of the journey. After many sessions of counseling, most of the mothers and women were prepared to testify against their abusers. We spent time building the case, and then it would be taken to court. We had a high success rate of 97 percent, which was a huge achievement in and of itself. The next step in our dream was to be able to expand on the home, to create more rooms so that we could house more people that needed help. And within eight months of opening the home, we were well on our way to achieving the expansion. It was turning into a small village, a village of support.

In between running the home with Sarah and overseeing the expansions, I spent a lot of time with Phil at the church. He would do his sermons, and I would be there to support him. Phil made sure to create a safe space within the church, we had an open arms policy, and anyone who needed to talk or feel safe was welcome at the church. We built a family outside of our own, and that was important. It was a big thing to make sure that people had a safe place to go. Most of the women and children from the home came to church, and through faith, they continued to grow in a personal capacity as well.

Five years later, Sarah and I had a successful support village. We managed to expand with an additional four buildings, which increased our capacity immensely. Most of the women that came through our doors made successes out of their lives. They were able to get jobs and a way to support themselves and their children. There was a handful that regressed over the years and ended up back with their abusers in the domestic violence cases, but we remained hopeful that they would come back and make the full change. The court cases were going well. It was very emotional to hear what these people had endured; how many children were sexually abused by family members and other adults. It solidified my resolve to expose the perpetrators and help the victims. I connected with every soul that came through the doors. Sarah and I were both given regular visits to our own therapists to ensure that our mental health was on track. All of this took a toll on us personally, but we had each other, and I'd learned that speaking about the things that bothered me made a huge difference.

I'd found my passion. I found where I wanted to be, and being there for people who were recovering was what God placed me on earth for. Survivors aren't alone. When we stand together, we grow. God gave me a huge family and the ability to make a difference, and I would continue to help until my time was finished. As Sarah and I got older, we made sure that there were people who were just as passionate as us to take over once we couldn't continue anymore, and I was confident that the home would continue for decades to come.

AFTERWORD

This book was written with the hope that it would inspire others who have been through similar experiences. My wish is that you will find the strength to follow your dreams and don't let go of them because of the tragedy that has happened. Trauma is a difficult thing to overcome, but you can do it.

Working through trauma or finding safety is hard. Walking away from a toxic relationship, family or friends, girlfriends or boyfriends, husbands or wives, is incredibly difficult, but don't be afraid to ask for help. You have the power to choose a better life. No matter how many times you've been knocked down, don't give up. Try one more time, and then again after that. Have faith in yourself and have faith in God. Take your power back, tell yourself that you can do it, that you deserve better, and don't underestimate the power of positive affirmations.

My closing words are: Find the strength to forgive those who hurt you. You have the power inside of you to accomplish your goals despite your past and your present circumstances. Take it one step at a time to be a better you. You may have to crawl before you walk. Walk before you run, but you will reach your goal. I have confidence that you will make it! God created you in his image; he doesn't create mistakes. You are beautiful, you are strong, and you are in charge. You are not alone; the moment you speak up is when your freedom begins. You are not a victim; you are a survivor.

I hope Naomi's story inspires you!

If you or anyone that you know is suffering from alcoholism, abuse, or mental health problems, please contact one of the organizations for additional information or if you are having a crisis. You are not in this alone:

- The National Alcohol Hotline: 1 866 977 9213
- The National Child Abuse Hotline: 1 800 422 4453
- The National Domestic Violence Hotline: 1 800 799 SAFE (7233)
- The National Suicide Prevention Hotline: 1 800 273 TALK (8255)

9780578289366